"The experience o
it is part of the hur
the modern age has greatly increased the opportunities and avenues of trauma. I'm thankful for Curtis Solomon and his good work in this book. You will be too."

Al Mohler, President, The Southern Baptist Theological Seminary

"*I Have PTSD* offers wise insights into how our bodies and souls respond to extreme suffering while offering the hope of the gospel for healing. Curtis compassionately breaks down the disorienting aspects of trauma and provides orienting biblical truths paired with practical steps to begin the healing journey."

Darby Strickland, CCEF Counselor and Faculty; author of *Is it Abuse?*

"In *I Have PTSD*, Curtis Solomon helps Christians rally the resources of their faith as powerful tools for regaining a sense of peace, stability, and hope. This is a great resource for believers wanting to know more of the Savior's comfort amid their struggle with trauma."

Brad Hambrick, Pastor of Counseling, The Summit Church, Raleigh-Durham, NC; author of *Angry with God*

"Curtis Solomon has compassionately combined practical advice with a biblical foundation, blessing us with this invaluable resource. This book will prove to be a wonderful tool for any counselor or sufferer seeking to offer or find hope within the disorienting realities of trauma."

Chris Moles, Pastor; author of *The Heart of Domestic Abuse*

"In this book, Curtis Solomon does a masterful job of providing both a clear perspective on trauma and PTSD and a biblical framework with practical steps for addressing it. This book is a hope-filled guide for anyone struggling through the challenges of trauma."

Jeremy Stalnecker, Cofounder, Mighty Oaks Foundation; author of *The Truth About PTSD*

"Have you suffered trauma? Are you an overwhelmed friend, family member, or church leader who needs guidance to help traumatized loved ones? This book is for you!"

Ellen Mary Dykas, Director of Equipping for Ministry to Women, Harvest USA; author of *Jesus and Your Unwanted Journey*

"Curtis's book on post-traumatic stress helps us lean in with curiosity, hope, and practical help. This book will become a faithful companion for complex struggles as you meet people in the darkest of places."

Jonathan D. Holmes, Executive Director, Fieldstone Counseling

"I am so thankful for this book which addresses a specific but common form of trauma and does so in a way that is deeply grounded in Scripture. I am certain it will prove to be a blessing to those who have endured such trauma and to those who are seeking to minister to them."

Tim Challies, Author of *Seasons of Sorrow*

"Solomon's wealth of experience with PTSD is constantly evident. It is realistic, rooted in Scripture, wise about physiology, full of case studies, and insightful about guilt, shame, and despair. *I Have PTSD* connects constantly back to the Lord and helps you construct a wise, holistic, and practical peace plan."

J. Alasdair Groves, Executive Director, Christian Counseling & Educational Foundation (CCEF); coauthor of *Untangling Emotions*

"If you're looking for a better understanding of PTSD, this is a must-read book that will help you, your loved ones, and those around you find hope through the gospel and pursue the life God intended for you!"

Chad Robichaux, Founder and CEO, Mighty Oaks Foundation; Force Recon Marine; JSOC operator; author of *Saving Aziz*

"People who suffer post-traumatic stress are exactly that—people who suffer. In this book, Dr. Solomon addresses you as a person, not a diagnosis or set of symptoms. He shows you the respect of a person made to know God in the complexities of your suffering."

Jeremy Pierre, Dean, The Billy Graham School of Missions, Evangelism, and Ministry and Lawrence & Charlotte Hoover Professor of Biblical Counseling, The Southern Baptist Theological Seminary; author of *The Dynamic Heart in Daily Life*

I HAVE PTSD

REORIENTING AFTER TRAUMA

Curtis Solomon

New Growth Press
newgrowthpress.com

New Growth Press, Greensboro, NC 27401
newgrowthpress.com

Cover Design: Studio Gearbox, studiogearbox.com
Interior Typesetting and eBook: Lisa Parnell, lparnellbookservices.com

ISBN: 978-1-64507-335-2 (Print)
ISBN: 978-1-64507-336-9 (eBook)

Library of Congress Cataloging-in-Publication Data on file

Printed in the United States of America

30 29 28 27 26 25 24 23 1 2 3 4 5

To Jonny.

My teacher, my friend, my brother.

CONTENTS

INTRODUCTION

Trauma invades life. It harms, destroys, and even kills. Anyone left alive after a potentially traumatic event feels confused, lost, out of control, unsure, and unsteady—disoriented. This book is written for people in that state. If you have faced intense suffering or love someone who has, then it's for you. Words are inadequate and most imaginations cannot fathom the kind of suffering I'm talking about—suffering which always leaves marks, sometimes on the body, but always on the soul, and often on both.

Disorienting is a good word to describe the impact of trauma. It leaves one feeling dazed. No book can solve your problems, take the pain away, or fix it, but this one is designed to help you reorient your life after you have been disoriented by trauma. Trauma is not something that can be undone, but it can be overcome. This volume and the people who journey alongside you as you suffer are not ultimate solutions, but they are a source of help and will point you to the One who is.

Genesis 1:31 assures us God created the world to be "very good"—perfect in fact. Humanity's first sin opened the door to trauma and it has been with us ever since. One rebellious choice by the first couple left their descendants susceptible to death and decay and prone to go their own wrong way (see Genesis 3). If you open the Bible to its first book, Genesis, you will read story after story of trauma inflicted and endured. Trauma did not take a break or disappear; it has been with us ever since. In each generation, people from every tribe and nation have experienced and inflicted trauma.

There is no way a single book can say all that could be said about trauma or completely resolve all the challenges you encounter as someone disoriented by it. But don't lose heart. There is hope and healing offered in these pages. I have seen transformation in the lives of those disoriented by trauma. That's why I wrote this book for you—someone who has suffered greatly. I want to help you get your bearings and reorient your life.

Each chapter is designed to address different aspects of the struggle with trauma, including grief, guilt, and how you can experience post-traumatic growth and transformation. The chapters are in an order I hope will prove helpful, but you may want to tackle particular chapters out of order to meet your most pressing needs first.

Allow me to make two points on chapter order. First, if part of your experience involves panic attacks, dissociative episodes, or other instances in which life and your body feel out of control, please review chapter 4, "Your Peace Plan," first. This will help equip you to address these problems promptly. I don't want you to have to wait until the end of the book to get some relief from these disruptive experiences. Second, while it is not an absolute rule, I do find it's helpful to address grief and loss before addressing issues of guilt. This approach will show you the compassionate love of Christ so that any call to deal with what you have or have not done wrong will be wrapped in a loving invitation from Jesus to come to him for rest from your burden of guilt and shame.

"POST" TRAUMA

This book is written for those struggling with Post-Traumatic Stress. Understanding that it is for those who are "post" their traumatic experiences is key. One of the first and most important steps to reorienting your life and healing after trauma is to no longer be facing trauma. If you have been traumatized by abuse, the first step to take is making sure you are not still in an abusive relationship. The truths in this book will still be helpful to you if you are, but your first concern should be to get out of the abusive relationship. Leaving an abuser is hard but it is important for your spiritual and physical health. Please, as soon as possible, reach out to someone you trust and ask for help. You can start by calling the National Domestic Violence Hotline at 800-799-7233 or by texting START to 88788. There are also great Christian ministries like Called to Peace that care for people in abusive situations. (Please visit https://www.calledtopeace.org/.)

If you are not in an abusive relationship, you could still be facing repeated traumatic events. First responders, military members, and medical care providers often encounter one traumatic event after another. Your situation requires careful consideration. Two questions to think about are these: First, are you currently experiencing any of the impacts of the traumatic events in your life? And second, is it possible, advisable, or necessary for you to change career fields?

Regarding the first question, you could be in one of three places. Either you aren't experiencing any negative consequences from the traumatic events you've lived through, or you are experiencing some and don't know it, or you are aware of the trouble you are having. If you have a role like those I mentioned and are reading this book, you are most likely in one of the last two categories—you know you are experiencing trouble, or someone near you sees your struggle and has recommended this book to you. If you are in either one of these places, this volume can help. You will learn some ways to deal with past trauma and can start to build resilience so you can better handle future trauma. The fact that you continue to face traumatic events, however, will make it challenging to fully heal and move forward.

If you are in a career field like those I mentioned and are not currently facing any trouble from past trauma, this book can help you build resilience against it. After all, many people, especially those in the first responder community, don't experience Post-Traumatic Stress symptoms until they quit, retire, or switch career fields. When faced with one emergency after another, it's common to press forward without ever processing. People tend to stay in alert mode, being constantly distracted by the next emergency. While many can live by this pattern for a while, it often catches up to them eventually. You, in fact, might notice that unprocessed trauma will gradually (or suddenly) come to the surface. I tell retiring police officers, firefighters, EMTs, and combat veterans to be on the lookout for things to start popping up as they slow down. It is helpful to prepare for change and not be caught off guard by it.

Now, for that second question I mentioned. Is it possible you need to change careers or do something else to break the cycle of traumatic events related to your work? Each person is unique and there is not a one-size-fits-all answer here. If you are experiencing the impacts of trauma or your family or friends suspect you are, I encourage you to reach out to a biblical counselor and begin assessing the wisest path forward for you. Involve your family, close friends, and spiritual leadership in the decision-making process. Though changing careers is not without difficulty, doing so may be the best thing for you.

Whatever has prompted you to pick up this book, I encourage you to reach out to a trusted friend to walk through the journey ahead alongside you. You are not meant to go through life, let alone trauma, alone. So ask someone you trust, who loves you and Jesus, to help. A pastor, a small group leader, a biblical counselor, or just a good friend can be a wonderful support for you. You don't have to get into all the details of your trauma yet, or maybe ever, with that person. But you should let them know you've suffered significantly and would like them to read through this book with you in support of your efforts to reorient your life. If you don't know anyone that you feel could serve in that role, please reach out to a biblical counselor. (You can visit https://partners.biblicalcc.org/counselor-map/ to find one.) Some now provide care via online video sessions.

One truth that will be repeated many times in this book is this: *you are not alone!* Having someone walk this journey alongside you will demonstrate that reality to you again and again. Such an individual will be a concrete reminder of that core truth, which is important since those affected by trauma often struggle to believe it.

INTRODUCING THREE PEOPLE DISORIENTED BY TRAUMA

Allow me to introduce you to a few people who I will mention throughout this book. Their names are Vanessa, Javier, and Carl. Each of them represents a real person whose life has been disoriented by trauma. Some of the details shared in their stories have been altered or are an amalgam of the experiences of several different people; nevertheless, their suffering, loss, trauma, and disorientation—as well as reorientation, restoration, and hope—are authentic.

Let's begin with Vanessa. Her big brother was a high school football star. One Friday night, during a game, a fluke incident sent his helmet flying from his head right before he collided head-on with a player from the opposing team. Vanessa (and hundreds of others) watched in horror from the sidelines as the team's athletic trainer, then a doctor from the stand, and ultimately the EMTs surrounded her brother on the field. They rushed him away in an ambulance. Later, when she arrived at the hospital with her parents, Vanessa learned her brother had not survived.

Sergeant Javier Sanchez was an Army Ranger who had multiple deployments in Iraq and Afghanistan. While he encountered many traumatic events, he is haunted by two in particular. He once escorted a wounded enemy combatant through a hospital full of people maimed by war. In a separate incident, he was trapped in a broken-down Humvee while enemy fire slowly compromised the ballistic glass in front of him. The whole time, he wondered whether the next bullet would break through and end his life. Javier survived, but his injuries led him to be medically discharged from the Army.

Carl was driving down the road when a car suddenly shot out in front of him. There was no time for Carl to stop, and he hit the side of the car at full speed. It turned out that the other driver's vision had been blocked by a line of traffic waiting to make a right turn, so he hadn't seen Carl's car driving in the lefthand lane. The airbags and other safety features of Carl's car saved his life and prevented any major injuries. But the same could not be said for the child in the back seat of the other car who died in the crash. Carl was cleared of all legal responsibility since the car accident had been the fault of the other driver making an illegal blind turn.

Vanessa, Javier, and Carl all experienced traumatic events and, like you, each ended up suffering and disoriented. We will revisit their stories throughout this book, so that you can see how—step by step—trauma can be overcome. While overcoming often involves a long journey, there is hope for healing and growth. These can come from the hands of the great Healer of soul and body—Jesus Christ.

A WORD FOR THE HELPER

If you are taking time to minister to someone who has suffered greatly, I thank you. This book is written for trauma sufferers, but also with you—the helper—in mind. Those coming to you for care may not be able to read this on their own. If that's the case, you can read it for them. Please use it as a guide as you offer counsel and support; its pages are packed with wisdom.

Remember, you are not alone. God is with you, I'm with you, the body of Christ is with you, and the person who is coming for care is with you. He or she is not just someone who needs help, but—I think you will find—can be a great source of encouragement, help, and wisdom to you as well.

Should you ever feel in over your head, know there's nothing wrong with reaching out for help. I'll guide you through developing a Transformation Team in chapter 1 and in resource 1: "Transformation Team Additions on page 118." Don't neglect the help offered by secular authorities to help in emergency situations. If someone you are caring for is a threat to themselves or others, don't hesitate to call 911 or 988 (the Suicide and Crisis Lifeline). But I want to remind you to pray more than anything else. Pray for the one you are caring for. Do so before each meeting to discuss this book. Do so during your time together. Do so anytime the one you're aiming to help comes to mind.

Be encouraged that by walking alongside someone disoriented by trauma, you are participating in Jesus's mission "to proclaim liberty to the captives and recovering of sight to the blind, to set at liberty those who are oppressed" (Luke 4:18). Jesus wants to set free those who are disoriented by trauma, and he will help you and them. Don't forget that the one asking for your help is not ultimately in your hands, but in God's. So call out to him, rely on him, trust in him.

PART 1

You Are Not Alone

Chapter 1
NEVER FIGHT ALONE

Sergeant Javier Sanchez awoke on the side of a dirt road. He could feel someone searching through his pockets for medication and another person doing a sternal rub, a technique he knew medical providers use to determine whether a person is conscious. For a moment he wondered what had happened. Then it came back to him. The van he'd been riding in had made a turn off a smooth blacktop road onto a gravel road. The sound of the gravel bouncing off the van's wheel wells had triggered his body's fight-or-flight response and he had passed out. It had reminded him of the time he was trapped in a broken-down armored Humvee, watching the ballistic glass in front of him deteriorate with each enemy round.

As Javier sat up, he looked around and reminded himself, *I'm in a safe place.* Many of the men with him in the van had been in a similar situation. Their response to his dissociative episode showed him they knew what it was like to walk in his shoes. He knew he was surrounded by other men who had gathered together to get biblical help for their battle with Post-Traumatic Stress (PTS).[1] The ministry called Mighty Oaks had been started by combat veterans to help other veterans whose lives have been disoriented by trauma. The ministry has since grown to reach out to first responders as well as the spouses of those impacted by trauma. The motto of Mighty Oaks is "Never fight alone."[2]

If you, like Javier, find yourself experiencing the long-term effects of trauma, that motto marks the place you must start the journey toward reorientation. *You are not alone*, and you really don't have to address what you're dealing with by yourself.

I don't know what you have been through, but I do know it was horrible. People don't read a book on overcoming trauma if something terrible has not rocked their world. But while your story is unique to you, I want you to know there are other people who have lived through terrors too. In fact, there is no segment of the population, no age range, no gender, no ethnicity, no socioeconomic status, that is beyond the reach of trauma. It is not a military thing or a law-enforcement thing; sadly, it is a human thing. Trauma happens on the battlefield and in the bedroom. It is linked to combat, car accidents, violent crime, natural disasters, abuse, and unexpected deaths of all kinds. Trauma leaves behind a wake of destruction. Many of its sufferers have physical scars to accompany the invisible ones. These show up in all kinds of ways, such as how we respond to certain scents, sounds, sights, and textures. Trauma can impact whole families and futures. It can crush dreams and happy memories of what was. Trauma disrupts the body, the soul, one's abilities and relationships, one's connection to creation, the concept of God, and even the desire to live. It leaves its victims disoriented, unsure of where to go, what to do, or what lies ahead.

If overcoming trauma seems like a mountain you can't climb, don't look at the whole mountain—just grab the first rock you can hold on to. It's labeled, *You are not alone!* Grasping that will give you a measure of stability as you start learning to reorient your life. It will be a source of hope and strength. By contrast, believing you are alone could cause you to slip deeper into despair.

YOU NEED A COMMUNITY

"But no one can understand what I've been through!" Does that sentence ring true for you? It commonly does among people who have been disoriented by trauma. The level of suffering you have faced seems rare and incomparable. But that is not true, and believing the lie will tempt you to isolate from the rest of the world and keep you from getting help. Throughout human history, people have been disoriented by trauma. But throughout history, people who have experienced trauma have also found hope and help. Their lives were reoriented, and they were able to move forward.

"Being alone with my thoughts was one of the worst places I could be," my Uber driver confessed one day. He was a former combat medic who still had shrapnel embedded near his spine to go along with his diagnosis of PTSD. It turned out the man didn't need to drive to make money. He drove to face his fear and to let strangers help him avoid isolation. I was impressed by his wherewithal, insight, and self-awareness. He hadn't been to counseling. He wasn't a Christian as far as I could tell. Nevertheless, he intuitively accepted the very thing God the Creator said at the beginning: "It is not good that the man . . . be alone" (Genesis 2:18). While isolation is not ideal for anyone, it is downright dangerous for those disoriented by trauma. As Joni Eareckson Tada puts it, "Community breeds life. Isolation leads to death."[3]

You need a community. You need people around you to help you walk through life. On a tough journey like the one you are on, there are particular people I want you to invite into your life. I will call them your Transformation Team.

These are the individuals who will walk with you through your suffering and encourage you to became more like Jesus—the One who will be your ultimate source of comfort and transformation.

YOUR TRANSFORMATION TEAM

Your team starts with you. You are reading this book because you want help and that is significant. But others—whom you *do* need—can't help you if you don't invite them along. So whom should you ask to help you? Below is a list of key members of the transformation team I urge you to begin assembling.

The Primary Biblical Counselor

The primary biblical counselor is the person who'll meet regularly with you. His or her role is to bring hope, help, and healing from Scripture. Ideally, this individual already serves in a shepherding role in your local church or is trained in biblical counseling. But don't be discouraged if you don't have someone like that in your life already. God works through all kinds of people, trained and untrained. And if you need help finding a biblical counselor, you can visit the Biblical Counseling Coalition's website: https://www.biblicalcounselingcoalition.org/. Your primary counselor can be a great resource in helping you build out the rest of your Transformation Team.[4]

Counseling Ally

The counseling ally is really just a close trusted friend. Ideally you will ask someone who is already a spiritual mentor to you and a mature believer in Jesus Christ to serve in this capacity. Your ally will attend counseling sessions but will not typically participate in the giving of counsel. His or her role is to support you while you are receiving counseling and to reinforce the counsel provided. Your ally can help you remember to do homework, remind you of wisdom offered in session, and provide encouragement and accountability between sessions. Your ally will serve as the first point of contact between sessions too.

There are many benefits to using allies in counseling. For one, the practice will deepen your relationship with your friend and help you both better realize the benefits of meaningful friendship. Having an ally will also help you fight the stigma that sometimes accompanies being in counseling. He or she will be a key part of having a healthy community around you that will continue long after formal counseling concludes.

Support Friends

Support friends are three to five other close friends whom you can ask for help. They don't need to know the details of your problems, and they will not attend counseling sessions. Rather, being equipped with your Peace Plan (something we'll discuss later), they'll be available for phone calls. Having support friends helps distribute the caregiving and ensures someone is always available to talk should you have a need arise. If you have a panic attack, need some extra encouragement, or just want someone to talk to you, your support friends can be just as helpful as your counseling ally.

Co-Sufferers

The Bible teaches that there is comfort in shared suffering. The apostle Paul wrote this: "No temptation has overtaken you that is not common to man" (1 Corinthians 10:13). I bring that up because the word translated "temptation" here can also be translated as "trial."[5] Trials and temptation go together. Temptations are times of testing and trial, and suffering tempts us in particular ways. Severe suffering and tribulations of all kinds have been prevalent since Adam and Eve disobeyed God. Through the centuries there have been many people who have lived through similar circumstances to yours and actually grew through their suffering. This is why it is so good to find some people who can demonstrate this truth to you through their own stories.

Finding someone who has been through something similar to you can make the truths of Scripture more real to you too. Such people can bring us hope in our suffering. Hope that someone understands what we have been through and what we are going through. Hope that there is the possibility of growth. Hope that there is the possibility of a future.

If you've already been talking to someone about your trauma, ask if they know others you could talk to who have been through experiences similar to your own. Then meet with that person and ask to hear the story of what they went through. How has it impacted that individual? How did they receive help? What growth has this person experienced since? Doing this can serve as a powerful source of hope and encouragement that will keep you pressing forward.

It might be a good idea to connect with a group of people who have also been through trauma. If you are a member of the military community (active, guard, reserve, or veteran), a first responder, or the spouse of someone in these fields, the Mighty Oaks Foundation has a free program you could attend.[6] GriefShare is another ministry that connects people who've experienced significant loss in their lives.[7]

Connecting to other people who can show you that you are not alone in your suffering is one of the best ways to let go of isolation and lean into the healing and growth God can provide.

God

The Lord promises never to abandon anyone who comes to him in faith (Hebrews 13:5–6). Even though you can't see him, he is with you and can offer comfort, encouragement, and help through many avenues. God cares for all his children, but he has a special concern for those who have suffered greatly. In both the Old and New Testaments, God declares his love and care for those who are afflicted. His compassion is expressed in being intimately involved with us—he enters into our suffering (Isaiah 63:7–9; Hebrews 4:15).

God's heart for sufferers is apparent all throughout the Bible, but one particularly encouraging passage is in Romans 8. In it, the apostle Paul doesn't try to ignore or minimize suffering. Instead, he highlights the widespread nature of suffering and demonstrates how it affects the whole world (vv. 19–22). While this is bad news indeed, Paul points out that we who trust in Jesus Christ as Savior are not left to suffer alone. In verse 26, Paul reminds us that the Holy Spirit "intercedes for us" when we are so overwhelmed with suffering and sorrow that we don't know how to pray ourselves. In verse 34, we also see Jesus, God the Son, interceding on our behalf. Do you know that the Lord himself prays for you every day, always?

At the close of chapter 8, Paul lists a variety of trials and sources of suffering in this life but concludes that none of them can separate us from the love of God which is available to us in Jesus. In Romans 8:35–39 he says this:

> Who shall separate us from the love of Christ? Shall tribulation, or distress, or persecution, or famine, or nakedness, or danger, or sword? . . .
>
> No, in all these things we are more than conquerors through him who loved us. For I am sure that

> neither death nor life, nor angels nor rulers, nor things present nor things to come, nor powers, nor height nor depth, nor anything else in all creation, will be able to separate us from the love of God.

God understands suffering. God understands *your* suffering. And he doesn't run away from it, but runs into it. He invites you to draw near to him, and he draws near to you (Hebrews 4:16; James 4:8). His primary means of doing so and communing with you is through his Word, the Bible. In it you will find wisdom for life, including help to reorient your life after trauma.

SUFFERERS IN THE BIBLE

Another way to know you are not alone in your suffering involves reading the stories of the Bible. It is full of historical narratives about people who experienced severe suffering. Genesis, the first book of the Bible, has several. In one, the first brothers in human history become the world's first murderer and innocent victim. Further in, another brother steals the family inheritance and runs for his life from his twin's murderous rage. Later, a young woman is raped and an entire city feels the wrath of her family. Her little brother gets sold into slavery by this same family, then is falsely accused and imprisoned. And this is only a taste of the drama you'll find in just the first book of the Bible.

An entire book could be devoted to recounting the traumatic experiences recorded in Scripture. The Bible does not fail to address trauma. It does not ignore the hard parts of life; rather, it puts them on full display. But know this as well: it doesn't just record traumatic experiences. It addresses the hearts of people disoriented by trauma, and it offers hope and help to them and to you.

My goal in writing this book is to help you reorient your life to be aligned with God's original design. In the pages ahead, we are going to look at ways your traumatic experiences have disoriented your life and seek to reorient them around God's love and care for you. Should you have any doubt about his feelings for you, remember how lavishly he expressed them in sending his Son Jesus to redeem you from your sin and make you his own.

QUESTIONS FOR REFLECTION, DISCUSSION, & ACTION:

1. Have you ever thought that no one can understand what you have been through? What other thoughts or feelings has trauma evoked in you?

2. How did what you read in this chapter address the thoughts or feelings you acknowledged in that first question?

3. How does knowing the Bible is full of the stories of sufferers impact you?

4. List the name(s) of anyone you've been able to share your suffering with to this point. Then list some people who might be able to walk with you in one of the ways described in the above section titled "Your Transformation Team." Reach out to each one, seeking their partnership.

Chapter 2

POST-TRAUMATIC STRESS: A COMMON RESPONSE

"I'm a freak."

"I am broken."

"I'm a monster."

"If people knew what goes on in my head, they would never talk to me again."

"Everyone would be better off without me."

These are just some of the thoughts that plague people disoriented by trauma. Other descriptions of the experiences common after trauma include, "I don't want to remember, but I can't forget," and "I don't want to forget what I don't want to remember." These expressions point to similarities in experiences. These similarities are the themes that led to the creation of the diagnosis of PTSD.

No two people, however, experience trauma in exactly the same way. Even people who live through the same event will have different responses and different wounds as a result. That's why the events that cause post-traumatic stress are called "potentially traumatic" rather than just "traumatic." Although no two responses are exactly alike, there are some common themes among people who experience trauma.

Some of those themes are used by psychologists to diagnose Post-Traumatic Stress Disorder (PTSD).

The diagnosis of PTSD requires that someone has experienced a particular type of event, known as a potentially traumatic event, and then developed certain behavioral symptoms. Those symptoms are grouped into four categories: intrusive, avoidance, cognition/mood alterations, and altered arousal reactivity.[1] The first category, intrusive symptoms, are those experiences in which something related to the traumatic experience breaks into the mind through dreams or flashbacks. Avoidance symptoms include the behaviors we employ to stay away from anything that reminds us of the trauma or ignites a threat response. Alterations in thinking and mood encompass many factors, including difficulty concentrating, irritability, and negative thoughts about self, others, and the world around us. Altered arousal reactivity includes things like exaggerated startle response (being extra jumpy) and always feeling in a state of alertness (hypervigilance). When these things persist for over thirty days and occur any time a month after the event(s) at their root, and the symptoms significantly disrupt life, then a sufferer can be diagnosed with PTSD.

I prefer to call the aforementioned responses *post-traumatic stress* (PTS) rather than *post-traumatic stress disorder*. Why? First, adding the word "disorder" to post-traumatic stress can communicate that you, the sufferer, are disordered—that you are somehow weaker, or lesser than others. Many people who are diagnosed with PTSD feel like something is inherently wrong with them. They worry they are weak, freakish, broken, or abnormal. One important truth I want you to take away from this chapter, then, is that your *experience of these symptoms is not an abnormal response to everyday life. It is a* common *response to extreme suffering.*

The second reason I prefer the phrase post-traumatic stress to post-traumatic stress disorder is that the disorder language tends to communicate that PTSD is a medical problem or disease. Some mental health care professionals will even say things like this: "You have PTSD, and there is no known cure." But this robs those who are suffering of hope, making them believe they are trapped in that horrifying state and there is nothing to be done about it. Importantly, this conception of PTSD is rooted in a worldview that accepts that the physical world is all there is. If people are just physical bodies as that implies, then when something goes wrong there must be a biological cause behind it.

There certainly is a physiological component to PTS (we will discuss that next). But you and I are more than bodies. Most importantly, each of us has a soul that will live forever. According to Job 19:26–27, 1 Corinthians 15:51–55, and Philippians 3:20–21, our resurrected bodies will one day be reunited with our souls post-death as part of God's promise of eternal life (John 3:16). Both our souls and our bodies, we must understand, were created by God. And denying this has catastrophic effects for humanity in general as well as any person disoriented by trauma. It ignores the fundamental realities of life and can rob us of the incredible resources available through God and his Word.

The amazing reality that you were created by God as a unique person—with both a body and soul that will ultimately live forever—means there is hope for you to develop and be transformed though your trauma. The complexity of human existence means our problems as well as the solution to our problems involve more than one narrow aspect of our nature. God, the Creator of all, is the only one who fully understands your struggle with trauma. He has given us wisdom in the Bible to help us reorient our lives after trauma. Although that might seem like an unattainable goal right now, leaning on God invites him to take your trauma and use it for good in your life and the world around you (see Romans 8:28).

These are a few of the reasons I will call the troubling experiences that disorient someone's life after they survive potentially traumatic events Post-Traumatic Stress or PTS going forward.[2] This recognizes the reality of the struggle without stigmatizing a sufferer, robbing him or her of hope, or undercutting opportunities for growth.

THE BIOLOGY OF PTS: THE OUTER PERSON[3]

How people respond to trauma includes more than physical response(s), but that doesn't mean we should ignore the body. To understand the physiological impacts of Post-Traumatic Stress, you need to first grasp the proper function of the body systems that can be negatively altered by traumatic experiences.

God created humans with a threat detection and response system that incorporates various aspects of the body. For instance, the brain has two parts that are involved. One part senses a threat and the other assesses it.

We often talk about the threat response system as the fight-or-flight system because that phrase describes two of the primary ways in which we tend to respond to threats. We fight to destroy or eliminate a threat, or we take flight in order to get away from it. There are other common ways in which we respond to threats, however. Conveniently, they too have labels that begin with "f:" freeze, fawn, and faint. *Freezing* is what we do when we don't think we can defeat or get away from the threat so we hope the threat just passes us by. *Fawning* is a tactic we use primarily with other people we find threatening. Simply put, it is an attempt to pacify the threat. *Fainting* is a way of dealing with a threat by going numb, mentally checking out, or even physically losing consciousness.[4] That last possibility in particular is a good reminder that multiple parts of our bodies are involved in threat detection and response: the cardiovascular system, the endocrine system, and the musculoskeletal system are all clearly at work in fainting.

It helps to realize your threat detection system is always active. It functions much like a passive-learning alarm system on a house or car. The part of your brain most responsible for threat detection brings together memory, sense perception, and feelings in a very close relationship. It is constantly scanning input from all your senses and comparing it to historical data of memory and emotion. You gather as much sensory data about an experience as possible in order to deal with any immediate threat but also to prepare you for a similar threat in the future. Involuntary threat-sensing starts in the brain.[5]

Do you remember the first time you noticed the bright blue flickering flame under some bars on top of that box in your kitchen? As a child, you had not yet stored the threat data warning you not to touch the stove, so you reached for it. One of two things happened in that next instant: you got burned or your mom intervened and gave you a scolding. Either way, your threat response system stored some important data. As a result, the next time you saw the stovetop's flame, your threat response system kicked in and warned you of danger so that you didn't bother to reach for it. You listened to the danger warning and responded by flying away from the threat. You may have even felt the perception of danger in your body as a faster heartbeat, changed breathing, or muscle tension. Any of the above were signs your body was preparing you for protective action.

Another part of your brain plays the important role of assessing threats. As you grew up and your brain developed, you realized that the stove in and of itself was not a threat. You learned to distinguish between the stove and the flame. At some point you may have had the experience of your heart racing when you heard the sound of the stove top lighting up but then you reminded yourself that the stove was not dangerous. Part of your brain sensed a threat from that early experience, but the other part assessed the situation and judged it as unthreatening. This is the part of your brain that does most of your active thinking. It is where you think and evaluate. It controls your ability to speak and make decisions. This part of your brain has the responsibility of determining whether something is actually a threat or not. It assesses things, then tells the threat-sensing portion of your brain to stay on alert or not.[6]

The avenue that processes sensory data connects to this portion of your brain fractions of a second after it hits the threat detection center. Most of us have experienced this connection at work when someone jumped around the corner and yelled, trying to scare us. This is an indicator that your brain senses a threat and prepares you to respond even before you can cognitively process the threat. If everything is working as it should, the threat assessment part of your brain sees a dark hooded figure holding a knife and leaves your threat response active and you run like crazy or let your martial arts training take over. On the other hand, if your threat assessment recognizes the figure as your twelve-year-old son trying to play a joke, it tells the threat system to shut down. (How you decide to deal with him is an entirely different decision you'll have to make!) But even if you assess a situation as not threatening, you can still feel the effects of the threat response activation. Your heart will race, your breathing will intensify, and you might feel a little shaky from the adrenaline coursing through your veins. Your body was prepared for action before you could cognitively process the threat.

Another thing that's helpful to know is that your body's threat response system can be damaged when it encounters overwhelming threats, repeated significant threats, or structural damage caused by physical injury. In Post-Traumatic Stress, the threat response system is often negatively altered so that it turns on when it shouldn't, doesn't shut down properly, stays on all the time, or may not come on at all.

What do I mean by saying the system turns on when it shouldn't? This is when someone is triggered by something that is not threatening.[7] Often this occurs when one is exposed to sensory stimuli associated with the previous traumatic experience, but sometimes the cause cannot be identified. I mentioned earlier that our bodies latch onto as much sensory data as possible each time we encounter a threat. When things are working properly and when we face more normal threats, our brains help sort out what was actually dangerous about the experience versus what was incidental to the threat.

To return to our earlier example, if you were burned by the stove's flame as a small child, you might have associated the stove itself with danger so that the next time you were in the kitchen you were frightened even when the gas wasn't on. If you burned your hand on the stove's flame in adulthood, however, you don't associate stoves with danger; rather, you accurately assess that the fire coming from the stove is dangerous. Following traumatic experiences, however, that kind of sorting process doesn't always happen. For example, a woman who was raped by a man wearing a particular aftershave may find herself in a state of terror the next time she passes someone at work who happens to be wearing that same scent. While she may realize the smell of the aftershave is not actually threatening, the threat detection center in her brain has flagged it as dangerous nonetheless.

For some people experiencing Post-Traumatic Stress, the connection between the threat detection and threat assessment portions of the brain can actually deteriorate.[8] (I'll discuss later how these alterations can be reversed through counseling.) Deterioration can cause a delay in the system recognizing a threat as dangerous or not and thus fail to treat the threat response appropriately.

Those who have their threat response systems "on" all the time are often described as hypervigilant. This can mean they are more easily startled than others or have an overly strong reaction to being startled. Negative alterations to our threat detection systems can also make it difficult to sleep. Chronic sleep loss can lead to many other problems. Having an overactive threat response can also lead to other physical problems like adrenal fatigue, digestive issues, and difficulty in concentrating.

Since it is the control center of the rest of the body, the brain plays the most significant role in PTS. But other parts of the body, like those I mentioned already, contribute to things like panic attacks, digestive issues, dissociation, and pain in various parts of the body that are associated with muscle tension.

All this to say, it is important for you to be aware that some of the physical issues you are experiencing now could be connected to your traumatic experiences. If you suspect that's the case, you should talk with your doctor about them and discuss their potential connection to your traumatic past. It's important to make note of such problems and pay attention to them. Sometimes they can serve as your first warning that problems in your soul are flaring up. Indeed, a case of acid reflux or a tension headache could signal that you need to address what you are thinking or feeling.

Although everyone is different, the great news here is that many physical ailments can resolve as you begin addressing the soul needs related to your trauma. As you begin to understand what God has to say about your beliefs and experiences, stress-related physical symptoms can be relieved.

PRACTICAL TAKEAWAYS

There are a few key concepts I want you to remember from our discussion of the biology of PTS. First, knowledge itself is helpful. Understanding what is going on with your body can be hope-giving and encouraging. The founder of the Mighty Oaks Foundation, Chad Robichaux, was a Force Recon Marine who had done multiple deployments to Afghanistan under the Joint Special Operations Command. While on one deployment, Chad began developing severe physical symptoms that he initially thought were evidence of some neurological disorder like epilepsy. When he finally called for medical evacuation, he was evaluated and diagnosed with severe PTSD and then medically discharged from the Marine Corps. He notes that the knowledge of what was going on did not solve all his problems, but it was a huge help.[9]

Another important takeaway is that *you are not a victim of your body or its response to trauma*. I say this for two reasons. One, there is hope that even the physical alterations that are observable in the brain of someone who has been disoriented by trauma can be reversed. Two, some people use their difficult pasts as reasons they cannot grow and change or as shields to keep people at a distance. Your trauma is real, with real effects. But I hope the truth that healing is possible will encourage you not to fall into these tendencies but to keep seeking out the care needed to help you work through the struggles you face.

THE INNER PERSON

The Bible describes human beings using the language of inner self and outer self. Even today, secular culture uses terms like *body* and *soul* to describe these different aspects of our existence. Indeed, the two are inextricably linked and have significant influence over one another. But as Paul notes, there is not always a direct correlation between the well-being of one and the well-being of the other. In 2 Corinthians 4:16, for example, he writes this with regard to Christ-followers: "Though our outer self is wasting away, our inner self is being renewed day by day."

Because these two aspects of human existence are so intertwined, however, we have hope that the healing of the soul can also have a healing effect on the brain. In fact, some current studies point to brain healing as a result of talk therapy, meaning just talking and listening can help it. This is good incentive to keep talking to God and listening to him in his Word, and conversing with your Transformation Team.[10]

CONCLUSION

Your response to trauma is unique because you are a unique person with a unique blend of genetics, relationships, history, thoughts, feelings, and desires. Nevertheless, while the difficult things are unique, they are not uncommon. So when you face them, remember you are not having an abnormal response to normal life; rather, you are living a common response to extreme suffering. I pray that the knowledge provided above gives you insight and hope. I also pray it helps you more deeply believe that *you are not alone*.

QUESTIONS FOR REFLECTION, DISCUSSION, & ACTION:

1. What are some of the ways your body reacts when frightened? If you can't identify any, begin to pay attention. Note what happens to your breathing, your pulse, your perspiration, and your muscles. Assess how a scare leaves you feeling afterward.

2. Respond to this statement: What you are experiencing is not an abnormal response to normal life but a common response to extreme suffering.

Chapter 3

HOW THE WORLD BECAME DISORIENTED AND HOW JESUS RESTORES

"I didn't have any thoughts of God when it happened, while I was living the moment," Carl said of the car crash that haunted his dreams. "But afterward I questioned whether or not he was real. If he is real, I felt anger toward him. How could a loving God allow me to kill an innocent child and leave me to suffer like this?"

Carl's questions about God are commonly expressed among people who experience trauma. Even for those who grew up in religious homes or have strong faith, trauma can shake up beliefs about the Creator and his character. But we must realize God "does no wrong" (Deuteronomy 32:4 NIV) and is at work even through trauma. He wants you to know that he is well acquainted with your suffering, suffers alongside you in it, and wants you to draw nearer to him in spite of it.

HOW DID THINGS GET THIS WAY?

What happened to our good world that set the stage for trauma to touch our lives? The figure below helps explain how God originally made things to function. His creation was beautiful in every way—everything worked in perfect unity and harmony. This diagram depicts what humans enjoyed in the beginning when God's creation was still in his original design.[1]

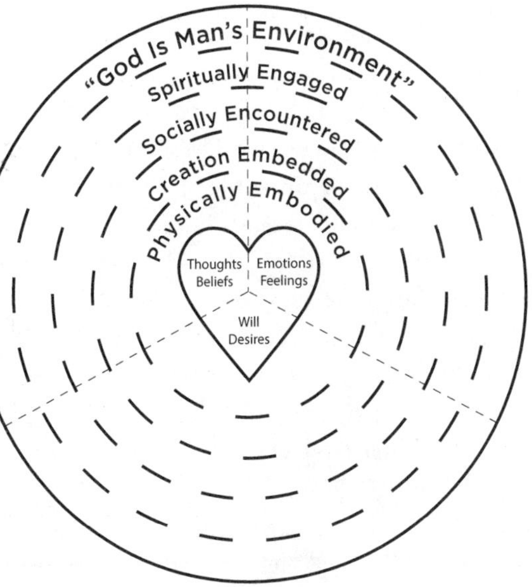

Let me explain what's happening in the illustration. Look at the center of the picture first. The Bible describes our inner person by using words like *soul* and *heart*, thus the heart shape. The inner person has three primary functions: it's the seat of our thoughts/beliefs—what we think; our emotions/feelings/affections; and our will—what we desire and choose. These things, of course, interact with and influence one another. For instance, if there is something we believe to be good, we want it, and we experience pleasant feelings when it's attained. On the other hand, if we believe something to be bad, we desire to avoid it, and get angry, sad, or afraid if we encounter it.

Remember, though, that we've never been mere souls floating around—we are embodied. Your body and soul are intimately and mysteriously intertwined. This is represented by the first circle surrounding the heart shape. The body and soul influence each other and interact. Moreover, we interact with all the other spheres represented above as well, influencing and being influenced by each.[2] We are embedded within creation. We encounter the world socially. We engage with God spiritually. All of this—the spiritual world, creation, all mankind (including us) exists in the presence of God and is sustained by his will (Acts 17:27–28; Hebrews 1:3). Even today, when things are functioning somewhat according to God's original design and our thoughts align with reality and truth, our feelings are entirely appropriate to the context, and our desires are right. We believers can even think God's thoughts, feel what God would feel, and know what God wants (1 Corinthians 2:16).

But when Adam and Eve turned their backs on God and went their own way (what the Bible calls sin), life was radically disrupted. As I mentioned previously with regard to Romans 8:19–22, everything fell under the curse of sin. And this is why human lives are currently disoriented from what God originally designed. People no longer naturally think what is true, seldom respond with appropriate feelings, and rarely desire to do what is right. The only things not disrupted by sin's impact are God and his sovereign rule over creation.

The following diagram illustrates the broken state of things within us now. Because of Adam and Eve's disobedience, each person begins life in this disoriented state. The presence of sin in our hearts and world, as well as the suffering we encounter further disrupts and disorients. If trauma is experienced, disruption and disorientation compound.

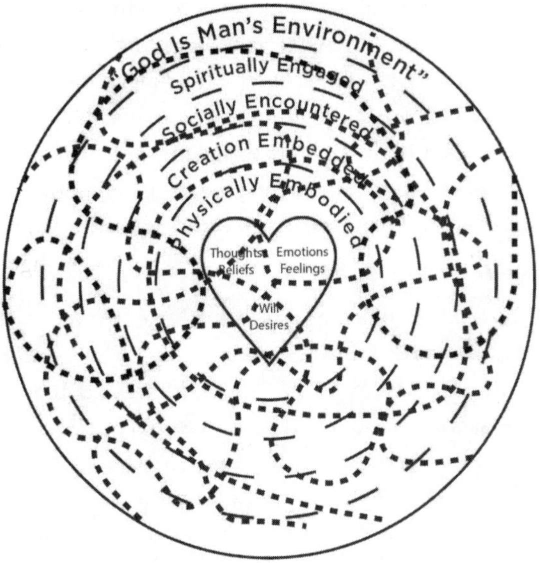

WHAT DID GOD DO TO HELP US?

When the first man and woman turned their backs on God, they brought suffering into this world. And ever since, trauma has been a possibility. Our loving God, however, didn't turn his back on them (or us). He made the human family a promise: one day he would send a Rescuer to save us from sin and its effects (Genesis 3:15). That Rescuer is Jesus Christ, who was born to a poor couple in a small village in Palestine. Yet he is God's own Son, our help and hope. Have you met him personally?

Perhaps that sounds like a strange question since it's been so long since Jesus walked on this earth. It could be that even the thought of Jesus sounds off-putting, bringing to mind an odd and aloof, handsome, fair-skinned guy in a white robe with a blue or purple cloth worn like a Boy Scout sash. But I want to challenge those ideas presented to us in movies. For one, this physical presentation is very different from the Bible's description of Jewish Jesus as having "no beauty" or anything else about his looks that would make him stand out (Isaiah 53:2). Second, though Jesus is often portrayed as being stoic, unmoved by human emotion, and unfazed by suffering until he encounters the cross, that is not at all the picture Scripture paints either. Jesus is your fellow sufferer.

Jesus—A Fellow Sufferer

The four Gospels, or parts of the Bible that tell the story of Jesus's life here on earth, describe a man who experienced great suffering (see Matthew, Mark, Luke, and John). The prophet Isaiah had foretold that Jesus would be "despised and rejected by men, a man of sorrows and acquainted with grief" (Isaiah 53:3). How was Jesus acquainted with it? What kind of sorrows did he endure? Why was he despised? And who rejected him?

From the beginning of his life on earth, Jesus was in danger. The king ruling his homeland was threatened by rumors of his birth in Bethlehem and sought to crush the threat of an incoming king by having all the infants Jesus's age and younger killed (Matthew 2:16). To save Jesus's life, his mother Mary and father Joseph fled with him to a foreign land, where they lived as refugees (Matthew 2:13–14).

It was not until around the age of thirty that Jesus began his public ministry. And those last three years of his life were marked by suffering.

- Jesus's own family initially rejected his teaching—mocking and ridiculing him (John 7:3–5). At one point, they even considered him "out of his mind" (Mark 3:21).

- Some essentially called him a bastard because his mother had become pregnant before marriage (John 8:41).
- The Jewish religious leaders, jealous of his abilities, accused Jesus of being demon possessed (Matthew 12:24; John 8:52).
- His cousin and ministry herald, John the Baptist, was brutally decapitated. Jesus didn't even have time to grieve because of the constant flow of people seeking his help (Matthew 14:1–13).
- Those in Jesus's hometown of Nazareth were so enraged by his (correct) claims to be the Rescuer God had promised that they tried to throw him off a cliff (Luke 4:28–29).
- For many months, Jerusalem's religious elites plotted to kill him (Matthew 12:14; 26:4; Mark 3:6; 14:1; Luke 22:2; John 8:59; 10:31; 11:53).
- He was betrayed into the hands of his enemies (mentioned above) by one of his closest friends. For a measly thirty pieces of silver (Matthew 26:14–16; 47–50).
- He was arrested and tortured for a crime he didn't commit. He was deprived of sleep, denied food and water, beaten, mocked, and carted back and forth between various illegal trials (Matthew 26:47–27:30; Mark 14:43–15:19; Luke 22:47–23:25; John 18:2–19:16).
- He was abandoned by his followers. One of his closest friends even denied knowing him (Matthew 26:69–75).
- The flogging he experienced was so brutal that it tore away flesh and muscle, likely exposing bone and internal organs. Many who experienced flogging did not survive it (John 19:1).

- Jesus was mocked and spit on and a crown of thorns was pressed down onto his head (Matthew 27:27–31).
- Jesus was crucified, which was a cruel method of execution designed to inflict as much physical pain as possible.

Yet in addition to all of this, Jesus had to bear the weight of the sins of the world while he was on that cross (1 Peter 2:24). The only truly innocent man who ever lived suffered and died so that we, the guilty, could live forever.

Jesus Christ endured more potentially traumatic events than any of us. And while in all his suffering he never sinned (Hebrews 4:15), that does not mean he was unaffected. The Bible never portrays Jesus as a stoic unmoved by emotion. He weeps when his good friend Lazarus dies (John 11:35). As mentioned, he desires alone time after learning of his cousin's murder. And Hebrews 5:7 says Jesus prayed "with loud cries and tears." This occurred "in the days of his flesh," a phrase broad enough to suggest multiple episodes. Particularly with regard to what Jesus experienced in Gethsemane the night before his crucifixion, the Gospel writers use deeply emotional language. He was in such anguish and distress that the blood vessels under his skin ruptured and blood flowed from his pores (Luke 22:44).

But Jesus endured all this suffering for a purpose. He did it to "become the source of eternal salvation to all who obey him" (Hebrews 5:9).

Jesus—Our Savior

The greatest sufferer in all human history endured the worst trauma imaginable to produce the greatest good—the destruction of sin and death and the eternal salvation of those who put their faith in him. Jesus gave his life in our place. Jesus, the innocent one, died for us, the guilty. All of us have gone our own way—all of us need saving (Isaiah 53:6; 1 Peter 2:25).

Now Jesus is alive forever. When the innocent died for the guilty, the power of death and evil was broken. The resurrection of Jesus from the dead was the start of something new. Now the broken, disoriented world can be set right, one person at a time (1 Corinthians 15:20–23; Ephesians 2:1–10; Colossians 2:13–15). Salvation by faith in Jesus doesn't just mean going to heaven one day. It means life and freedom right now (John 10:10; Galatians 5:1).

If you have not yet received this salvation, he offers it freely to you now. All you have to do is admit that you are a sinner, that he died in your place and rose again, and ask for forgiveness. Your God will forgive you and welcome you home (Romans 6:23; 10:9–11; 1 John 1:8–9).

If you have received the gift of salvation, he has another invitation for you. Hebrews 4:16 says, "Draw near to the throne of grace, that we may receive mercy and find grace to help in time of need." The risen Jesus understands your suffering better than anyone else ever could, even you. He doesn't push you away. He invites you to come to him for mercy and help. He has the power to bring healing and lasting change to you.

FOUR THINGS TO REMEMBER

Please hang on to four points from this chapter. First, ever since Adam and Eve went their own way instead of listening to God and following him, the world has been disoriented. Second, God nevertheless chose to rescue the world and put all things right. That's what the coming of Jesus was all about (John 3:16).

Third, Jesus understands your suffering because he has suffered—to the extreme. That means he can be empathetic toward you. No one knows your sorrow like Jesus. So draw near to him and receive grace, mercy, help, healing, and hope.

Fourth, God can (and does) bring beauty from ashes, treasure from trash, transformation out of trauma. After all, the greatest evil, the greatest trauma ever inflicted, was the murder of Jesus—the innocent, loving, perfect God come to earth as a man. But that evil brought about the greatest good: the salvation of all who would believe in him. As followers of Jesus, you and I can see this same pattern of death followed by resurrection in our own lives. This means that God can work through even the worst parts of your life—your trauma—to do amazing things in and through you.

QUESTIONS FOR REFLECTION, DISCUSSION, & ACTION:

1. How did this chapter inform or change your beliefs about Jesus?

2. How does knowing that Jesus suffered greatly, in part so he could sympathize with you, impact how you feel toward him?

3. If God is in the habit of working good through evil things, what does that imply for you and your situation?

PART 2
Dealing with Your Past

Chapter 4
YOUR PEACE PLAN

Remember Sergeant Javier Sanchez, who woke up on the side of the road after blacking out? Let's unpack what happened to cause his blackout. One minute he was riding in a van, chatting amiably with someone, the next he was waking up on the side of the road with his friends checking on him. Upon reflection, Javier recognized that one of the potentially traumatic events he'd encountered in combat involved being stuck in a vehicle, pinned down by enemy fire, and watching the glass in front of him become increasingly compromised with each enemy round. The bullets had made a *tink, tink, tink, tink* sound as they bounced off. When the van transitioned to a gravel road, it started kicking up rocks into the wheel well. The sound of the rocks bouncing off the van reminded his threat detection system of the prior traumatic experience. It went into overdrive and he passed out as a result. His experience highlights the phenomenon we often call triggers.

You can probably relate to being triggered by certain nonthreatening sounds, smells, or sights. Though they are not actually dangerous, they might still activate your threat response system as they remind you of a situation in which you were in danger. But other times you may feel a stress response and have no idea why. Understanding your triggers, to the best extent you can, will help you develop a plan to deal with them. Once this is established and shared with them, your Transformation Team will be better prepared to help you continue to reorient your life in a healing direction.

It can be comforting to know that people disoriented by trauma often experience varying degrees of distress. Distressing responses include panic attacks and dissociative episodes.[1] These can happen when the threat response system is initiated. A *panic attack* occurs when this threat response goes into overdrive. The person experiencing one feels out of control; his or her heart races and breathing normally becomes a challenge. Intense responses to triggers are always very distressing all by themselves. In the moment, it can feel like you are powerless against them. But now, while you are calm, you can take steps that will help you regain peace even in moments of panic and paralyzing fear.

DEVELOP A PEACE PLAN

A Peace Plan is designed to help you reestablish peace with God and with your inner and outer person. It invites God and others to aid you in the pursuit of peace. The basic steps are intentionally simple but profoundly helpful. Pray. Recline. Breathe. Think. Call.

The name "Peace Plan" is drawn from Philippians 4:4–9, which provides us great wisdom for battling anxiety and claiming the peace God provides. The passage says this:

> Rejoice in the Lord always; again I will say, rejoice. Let your reasonableness be known to everyone. The Lord is at hand; do not be anxious about anything, but in everything by prayer and supplication with

> thanksgiving let your requests be made known to God. And the peace of God, which surpasses all understanding, will guard your hearts and your minds in Christ Jesus.
>
> Finally, . . . whatever is true, whatever is honorable, whatever is just, whatever is pure, whatever is lovely, whatever is commendable, if there is any excellence, if there is anything worthy of praise, think about these things. What you have learned and received and heard and seen in me—practice these things, and the God of peace will be with you.

The most important and powerful aspects of the Peace Plan come directly from the wisdom this passage offers.

Pray

In this passage, the apostle Paul says that when we are anxious, we should pray and the result will be "the peace of God" guarding our "hearts" and "minds." That's why the first step in the Peace Plan is to pray. No, this does not need to be some elaborate and lengthy prayer filled with theological words. "God, help me!" is a great place to start. Elsewhere Paul writes something that we should keep in the back of our minds: "[T]he Spirit helps us in our weakness. For we do not know what to pray for as we ought, but the Spirit himself intercedes for us" (Romans 8:26). This is wonderful news because often when recalling or reliving the worst moments of our lives, we can feel unsure what to say. What a gift to know that God doesn't need our descriptions, though he welcomes them. So don't overthink things. Just turn your heart toward God in moments of panic, whisper for help if you can, and give him room to take over.

Recline

To recline simply means to sit down or lie down. I suggest doing so in moments of panic because there are a few things going on physiologically that need to be counteracted. Increased heartrate and shortness of breath can lead to dizziness, fainting, and in some cases more serious cardiovascular problems like cardiac arrest and stroke.[2] Sitting down or lying down can help counteract some of these symptoms and keep you safe.

Breathe

Proper breathing also helps counteract the physiological activity taking place during a panic attack. People experiencing panic attacks often take quick, short, shallow, gulps of air through their mouths. Rapid heart rate is a central physical component of the threat response system. Breathing and heart rate are directly linked. While you cannot voluntarily control your heart muscle, you can slow it down through the way you breathe.

Let's take a look at how to breathe properly. When told to take a deep breath, many people will lift and try to expand their chests. Proper breathing, by contrast, draws oxygen in using the diaphragm and will utilize the stomach muscles more than those in the chest. So when you inhale, draw your stomach muscles forward, away from your spine. When you exhale, pull those muscles in toward your spine. Also, when you inhale, draw oxygen in through your nose. When you exhale, release the breath through your mouth. Ideally, we should breathe this way all the time.

When panic strikes, you can respond to it in part by using proper breathing form, forcing yourself to take long, slow breaths. One technique for doing this is known as *box breathing* or *4x4x4 breathing*. To use this technique you'll inhale for four counts, hold for four counts, exhale for four counts, and hold for four counts. Each count lasts just under one second. Try it now, using the diagram below for reference. Just start at Step 1. Repeat the cycle four times.

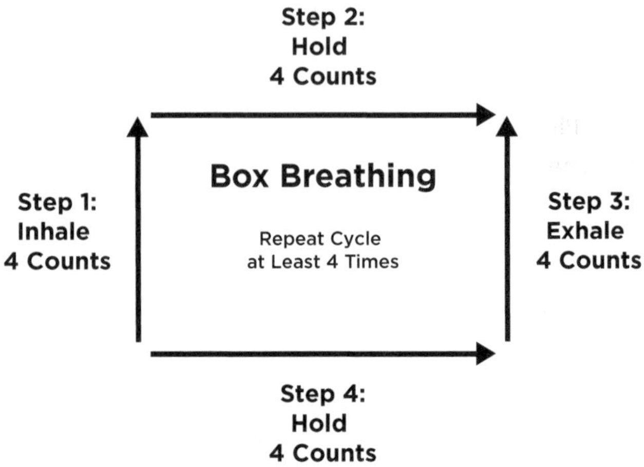

If you're finding it difficult to track your counts, try the exercise again. But this time, tap out the counts with your finger or your hand as you do. There are also many free apps available to help. One I often recommend is the Breathing App. It uses both audio and visual cues to help people slow and control their breathing. The visual cue is an expanding gray ball, almost like a balloon, which fills up as you inhale. As you exhale, the ball shrinks down. The audio cue involves two different tones, one to indicate inhaling, the other to indicate the exhale. The audio will allow you to close your eyes if doing so helps your focus. Users can also choose to utilize both the audio and visual cues simultaneously.

It is important to practice this breathing technique when you feel calm. This will equip and prepare you to use it in times of distress. Try doing some more box breathing now, or download the breathing app to see whether its cues are helpful for you.

Think

Breathing, of course, does not address the root of fear, even though it can address physiological reactions to it. To tackle fear at its source, you have to address your inner person. One way to do this is to think through and actually apply Philippians 4:8: "[W]hatever is true, whatever is honorable, whatever is just, whatever is pure, whatever is lovely, whatever is commendable, if there is any excellence, if there is anything worthy of praise, think about these things."

One component to fighting anxiety is learning to control our thoughts. Choosing to think about what is true, honorable, just, pure, lovely, and commendable is a great way to do that. I'm not suggesting you try to reason away your fear. I am urging you to trust God's Word and wisdom. During a panic attack, you'll need to find and cling to responses to these questions:

1. What's a truth about God? (Ex: "God is with me.")
2. What's a truth about me? (Ex: "I am not alone.")
3. What's a truth about my circumstances? (Ex: "I am not in danger.")

Notice that some simple truths include all three, for instance, "God is with me" could fit into all three categories. Here are some more thoughts you can use:

"God will never leave me."

"Be still and know that I am God" (Psalm 46:10).

"What happened in the past is not happening right now."

"This thing is not dangerous."

"I am safe."

Take some time now, while you are calm, to pick three to five simple truth statements that offer you hope and comfort. Some of them may be whole Bible verses. I've provided you space to write them here.

Truth Statements:

1. ______________________________

____

2. ______________________________

____

3. ______________________________

____

4. ______________________________

____

5. ______________________________

____

Call

Whenever possible, avoid facing trials alone. Should you begin to feel fear rising and panic taking over, begin with the steps above. But then call someone on your Transformation Team for backup. Each of them should be aware that you might call at any moment and be familiar with the Peace Plan I'm describing here. These friends can pray aloud for you, help count off your breathing, and remind you of the simple truths you have identified as most helpful for you. Please list Transformation Team names here for easier recall later.

People to Call

1. ______________________________

____

2. ______________________________

____

3. ______________________________

____

4. ______________________________

____

5. ______________________________

____

Be aware that it will prove hard, if not impossible, to execute a Peace Plan during a panic attack unless you have prepared and practiced it beforehand. So take some time now to make sure you have the above steps in mind and good people in place. And don't forget: Pray, Recline, Breathe, Think, Call.

IDENTIFY TRIGGERS

Now that your Peace Plan is in place, the next thing to do is to list all your known triggers. It is best to do this with a counselor or trusted friend who is part of your Transformation Team. For some, just thinking about triggers can ignite the threat response system, so having an ally nearby can help. You can write triggers down on paper or type them into your phone, but what's most important is sharing them verbally with the whole Transformation Team. If certain sights, sounds, smells, textures, feelings, people, or situations come to mind here, you will benefit from having others aware of it.

Often triggers bear a strong resemblance to some aspect of a traumatic event, but not always. One of my friends who struggled with anxiety, for instance, recognized a connection between his heart rate elevating as he worked out with the elevation of his heart rate during panic attacks. He noticed that the other feelings associated with anxiety would come up when he went to the gym. His anxious feelings had nothing to do with working out; nevertheless, his threat response system made a connection to the elevated heart rate.

When you find yourself being triggered without any known reason, take some time (usually after you have calmed down) to evaluate the situation. Doing this with a counselor or friend can be helpful because sometimes they will recognize things you haven't. If you can't get to the bottom of things right away, don't worry. Instead, create a log of such incidents in hopes of seeing patterns (see and work through Resource 2). Identifying patterns will enable you to turn your unknown triggers into known. Keeping your log—either on paper on in your phone—gives you constant and immediate access to it. You may even want to create voice memos on your phone—recording your answers to the questions posed in Resource 2.

Another helpful source of knowledge is your friends and close family—those who are around you daily. Sometimes they will notice you being triggered even when you don't. A friend who was a Navy Seal shared with me how his wife noticed that in certain situations he was acting stressed out. He hadn't recognized that personally, but her pointing it out helped him realize those situations were similar to a particular incident he'd encountered in combat. With his wife's help he was able to identify what had been an unknown trigger and then begin to work through it.

ADDRESSING TRIGGERS

"Knowing is half the battle!" G.I. Joe taught that slogan at the end of every episode of his 1980s cartoon. But in terms of knowing your triggers, having knowledge leaves the harder half of the battle yet to be fought. So, once you have listed your triggers, it is time to think about how you are going to handle them. Your Peace Plan is an important part of the process. But you will also need to expand its list of truths to remember. Take your list of known triggers, then, and write down a true statement about each one and its threat status. I've provided a couple of examples:

Trigger: Debris on the side of the road
Truths: Not all debris indicates an IED.
There has never been an IED attack along my route to work.
There is no reason an IED attack would happen within my neighborhood.

Trigger: Crowds
Truths: Not every crowd contains a threat.
I don't have to assess every person in this crowd for risk.
All these people are in God's hands, not mine.

One of the things trauma does is convince our threat detection systems that things which are actually safe are dangerous. It is impossible to instantaneously shut down your threat response system when it senses a threat. However, with time and practice, you can begin to alter the threat detection system's response to certain stimuli and learn to detect true threats without growing frightened by things that are safe. This starts by meditating on truth in the manner I've discussed, and having others speak truths to you with regard to your triggers. So, if you haven't already done it on your own, work with a friend or biblical counselor to create a list of truths related to each of your triggers.

Let us consider what this exercise would look like for Vanessa, whose brother was killed in a tragic football accident. She becomes overwhelmed with fear every time she sees someone wearing a jersey or shirt from her brother's team. Vanessa could choose to start responding to such sights with a statement like this: "Those jerseys are not harmful." Or, "Those jerseys remind me of something sad, but they didn't make that sad thing happen." She may even say, "That jersey is not going to hurt me or anyone else."

Now let's think about what this would look like for Carl. After his car crash, just getting behind the wheel of a car ignited his threat response. For a while he couldn't even drive. Carl had to begin reminding himself of truths related to driving and his crash. His counselor helped him choose some nuanced truths because just saying "Driving isn't dangerous" was not a completely honest statement. So he started with truths like these. "Sitting in a car is not dangerous." "Many people drive safely every day." "What happened on that day is not likely to happen today." Carl, though, was particularly helped by working theological truths into his trigger truths. He liked thinking, *My life and safety are in God's hands*, and *God is ultimately in control of traffic*.

One dual trigger truth that almost everyone who struggles with PTS needs to adopt is this: "That bad memory is in the past; it is not in the present. What I went through then is not happening right now." Another, along the same lines, is this: "Memories can be painful, but they can't hurt me now."

Once you've made your list, review it periodically so that you are regularly reminding yourself of those trigger truths when you are calm. It will make it easier to bring those truths to mind when you need them. Then, when you begin to sense fear or panic, you can work your Peace Plan and include the thoughts regarding any particular triggers that are present.

When you know you are going to be exposed to a trigger or potential trigger, you can pray beforehand to ask God to give you peace, help you maintain control, and to help you remember the truth about that trigger. You can also invite your Transformation Team to pray for you in advance and put them on alert that you may soon call.

AVOID AVOIDANCE FOR AVOIDANCE SAKE

It is common—and completely understandable—for people to try to avoid those things and situations that evoke painful memories and emotions. It is also entirely appropriate for people to take time away from normal life to grieve and heal after significant loss. But trauma often leads us to isolation and inactivity in our attempts to avoid anything that might remind us of the traumatic experience or evoke those painful memories and emotions. Isolation and inactivity only compound the struggles associated with PTS. Isolation, after all, removes you from others who love you and can help you. Inactivity tends to increase thoughts and feelings of being worthless, having no purpose, or being broken and damaged with no hope for healing. Just sitting alone with your thoughts can be dangerous. It's important to accept that trying to avoid all your triggers will only allow fear to grow. Fear of the fear will grow as well.

But how can you move forward when you feel paralyzed? First, recruit others to help you with this—ask for prayer regarding specific situations and triggers. Then ask someone to help you evaluate your list of triggers and divide them into two groups: the necessary and unnecessary.

Necessary triggers are the ones you'll need to face in the normal day-to-day. These could include driving to work, returning to your crowded church, or having sex with your spouse. For Vanessa, returning to school in spite of the memories the place evoked was a necessary trigger. For Carl, driving was a necessary trigger because he worked in an office downtown. Javier noted that the sounds of screaming children would often trigger memories about the wounded children he'd seen in hospitals in Iraq. But because he was a father to young kids, he'd likely keep having to deal with that particular trigger, which meant putting it on his necessary list.

Unnecessary triggers are the ones that don't have much to do with day-to-day life. I'm talking about things like seeing or wearing a particular outfit, encountering a certain meal or fragrance, or visiting a location that is not part of your normal routine. If Vanessa's brother had died at an away game, going to the football field where the accident happened would be an unnecessary trigger. Doing so is not part of her normal life routine.

Once you have all your triggers broken down into the two categories, identify the most frequently occurring necessary trigger and think through the ways in which you are commonly exposed to it. (It is helpful to do this with a biblical counselor or someone on your Transformation Team.) Consider the time(s) of day that normal life would most likely require you to deal with it, where that would occur, who if anyone would be around at that time, and how you respond to that trigger. Try to be as comprehensive and specific as you can. Consider your inner-person and outer-person reactions. What thoughts, feelings, or desires do you have? Do such encounters make your mind go blank? Do they flood you with images or other sensations from the traumatic event?

What happens to your breathing? Your heartrate? Do you begin to sweat? Do you feel lightheaded? Do you feel hot? Do you begin to shake? Do you experience muscle tension or pain anywhere?

Once that's done, think about how you would like to respond in those situations instead. For Javier, his child's screams following a tumble on the playground leave him feeling overwhelmed and paralyzed. His fists clench and his muscles tighten. But he wants to respond calmly and move with compassion toward his daughter to help her instead.

Take a moment to think about what you would like your goal response to a certain trigger to be. Then pray and ask God to help you (James 1:5). Next, write down your goal response to share with your Transformation Team. Then, since you can be certain you are going to encounter that trigger in the near future, ask God to prepare your heart to respond in the way you hope and ask your Transformation Team to do the same. Later, when you first encounter that expected trigger and begin to feel your typical threat response kick in, execute your Peace Plan. Pray. Breathe. Call. Think. The person you call should be prepared to add your goal response to the encouraging truths he or she can remind you of.

Don't be surprised or discouraged when you still become distressed by your triggers. Changing our reactions often takes time and practice. After all, you have involuntarily added certain undesirable responses, and possibly voluntarily added compounding undesirable responses to them. It takes time to unlearn those things.

Now, intentionally entering situations in which you know you'll encounter necessary triggers is another helpful tool.[3] Doing this with the help of a supporter and doing it in small increments is wise. For instance, Carl might sit in a car's driver's seat with his biblical counselor or a trusted friend beside him. Before they get into the car, however, he should first ask God for the peace that "surpasses all understanding," which only God can provide (Philippians 4:7). Once in the car, Carl can mentally picture driving someplace familiar. Meanwhile, both he and his ally can monitor Carl's responses by making note of the reactions and their severity throughout the brief experience. At any point, Carl or his friend can bring in elements of his Peace Plan to help Carl maintain self-control and avoid being overwhelmed by fear or panic.

The central element of the Peace Plan is turning to God, remembering that he is always with you, that nothing can happen to you outside his control and that he is your "helper" (Hebrews 13:5–6). As you ask for help, remember that all three members of the Trinity pray on your behalf (Romans 8:26–39) and the Holy Spirit can take over when you don't know what to say to God (Romans 8:26). Those who have been disoriented by trauma know that experience better than most. Your prayer may only consist of, "God, help me!" or perhaps even those words fail and all you can do is turn your thoughts to him as you otherwise groan in the agony of your suffering. Right then, he is with you and will pray for just what you need (Romans 8:23–26).

After mentally driving his route over and over with his ally, Carl will likely experience less distress over thoughts of driving. At some point, he—preferably with someone from his Transformation Team—can get behind the wheel of the car and actually start driving. But these first short drives should be prayed over in advance and the Peace Plan should be reviewed and kept in mind each time. As Carl drives, his friend should monitor him for any signs of distress and ask how he's doing on the inside. When Carl becomes distressed, he will need to utilize elements of his Peace Plan, including praying more and thinking about what is true. If, however, his distress rises to the point to which it is unsafe to be on the road, he should pull over and seek to calm with God's help and the help of his friend. If he can regain composure, Carl can finish the drive, but he may need his friend to drive him home.

The friend needs to be on the alert for whatever false thoughts Carl is wrestling with. He or she can establish and share truths to counter them. These should be added to Carl's truth list. Some false ideas that commonly plague people disoriented by trauma are these: "It's no use," "I'll never get better," "Why should I even try?" It is helpful when a supportive friend can calmly counter these thoughts with truths from both his or her own experience and from what the Bible says. Another thing the friend can do is remind Carl of how much progress has been made. He might say as he drives Carl home, "Hey, don't forget that last week you drove for fifteen minutes and then you pulled over. This week you drove for *forty-minutes* without stopping once." Hearing Philippians 1:6 could be very helpful to Carl too. It says, "I am sure of this, that he who began a good work in you will bring it to completion at the day of Jesus Christ." This verse directs our attention to God as the source of true growth in our lives. It's also a reminder that each of us remains a work in progress throughout this life. Nobody will be perfect until they come face-to-face with Jesus in eternity (1 John 3:2).

Here are some points to keep in mind as you work through this process. First, as you start working through your list of triggers, don't try to tackle the whole list at once. Take things one at a time. Second, always remember that the Bible invites us to lean into God's strength and sufficient grace, which are powerfully present in the midst of weakness (2 Corinthians 12:9). Third, though as time goes on you will experience a gradual decrease in negative response to your triggers, it probably won't be a steady, smooth decline. There will likely be seasons in which you experience an increase in the struggle—especially when you feel tired, are dealing with a season of great stress, and often around the anniversary of a traumatic event. Don't lose heart, don't be shocked, and don't believe all the work you've done has been in vain. Be kind to yourself, seek the support of God and your Transformation Team, and return to your Peace Plan.

AVOIDABLE (UNNECESSARY) TRIGGERS

Now, what are you to do about your avoidable triggers? These are situations and activities you don't *have* to face in the normal course of your life. When it comes to these, there is less need to tackle them directly or quickly; nevertheless, there is wisdom in addressing them as well.

On one hand, there is no requirement that you face every scenario that reminds you of traumatic events—especially those that don't hinder you from living the life God has called you to. Many people don't want to face the distress and pain of confronting triggers that they will likely never encounter in the normal course of life. Vanessa, for instance, may choose never to go to the exact football field where her brother died. It was not at the school she attended, her work does not require her to go near there, and she isn't letting anyone down or failing to fulfill any responsibility by not going.

But on the other hand, avoiding for the sake of avoidance can allow fear of the fear to grow, as I've pointed out previously. Some people, then, choose to face everything that triggers them. They don't want anything to control them or prevent them from encountering any part of life.

Whether you confront unnecessary triggers or not is up to you. This is a decision that takes much prayer, discernment, and should be made in the context of wise counsel from loving friends. Such people can encourage and support you should you choose to face the things that remind you of the worst moments of life. But they should never force the issue.

CONCLUSION

Your life has been disoriented by trauma. One of the significant sources of that disruption are the triggers that initiate your threat response. They might simply make you feel afraid, or they could take your mind back to the worst moments of your life. But you are not helpless against them. They do not have the ultimate say or power over you. God promises to be with you as you face your triggers, and he has given you allies in that fight. You have his Spirit to pray with and for you, his Word of truth to find comfort in, and his people to walk alongside you. Learning to lean into him and the resources he has given will help you put fear back in its proper place.

QUESTIONS FOR REFLECTION, DISCUSSION, & ACTION:

1. What feelings did this chapter's content evoke? Did thoughts of confronting your triggers upset you? Were you excited at all by the prospect of overcoming?

2. To date, who has been the most helpful person in your fight against your triggers? Consider sending that person a note or text just to express appreciation.

3. What trigger would you like to address first? What will be the best part of gaining victory over that trigger?

Chapter 5
GRIEVE YOUR LOSSES

Trauma involves loss. Sometimes our losses are tangible and obvious. Carl (although accidentally) inflicted the loss of a child. Sergeant Sanchez lost his best friend Jake. Vanessa lost her brother. Other losses are less tangible but still very real. As I've mentioned, Carl lost the freedom to drive without fear. Sergeant Sanchez lost a sense of authority and command of his life. Vanessa lost the joy of watching football with friends and family. If you were to explore any traumatic event in any person's life, you would find a long list of losses associated with it. When we broaden the scope to include all the suffering one encounters in life, the losses that individual wrestles with pile higher and higher. So what are we to do with all that loss, all that suffering, and all that trauma? God has given us one particular way to deal with loss. It's called grieving.

But what does it mean to grieve, and why must we do it? Many people have been influenced by Elisabeth Kubler-Ross's work on grief. In several of her books, she identifies five stages associated with it: denial, anger, bargaining, depression, and acceptance.[1] She first applied this list to how people process the approach of their own deaths, but then also applied it to grief from loss in general. In his excellent book on grief, *God's Healing for Life's Losses*, Robert Kellemen demonstrates how this widely accepted five-stage model of grieving can only leave us with acceptance of the circumstances, while the grief process that God gives is designed to draw us closer to him and to transform our suffering.[2] The biblical process Kellemen lays out starts with being honest with yourself about whatever difficulty, pain, and suffering you've endured. Next, you are to take those sorrows to God and tell him all about the losses, suffering, and pain you are enduring. Then you move from expressing the pain to crying out to God for his help and comfort. As he brings comfort to you, though, he often does so *in* your pain, not through the removal of it. Your trust in God, in fact, grows as you wait on him and continue to weep with him through the pain.

How do we learn to grieve this way so that we grow in faith? It starts with learning to lament.

LAMENTING YOUR LOSSES

Throughout my years of counseling, I've found that many people have ungrieved losses that significantly inhibit their healing or growth. And although grieving is a key aspect of life, many do not know how to do it well (or at all). Lamenting is perhaps the most significant part of the grieving process. Lamenting is the action of bringing our griefs and sorrows to God. It is a dominant theme of the Psalms, and it is one that should permeate the lives of Christians. The key aspect of lamenting that sets it apart from mere complaint or self-pity is the direction of the heart. When we lament, we don't simply declare our complaints and we don't weaponize our feelings against those who inflicted the harm. Instead, we take all our sadness and loss to God and seek to honor him through it all.

I need to emphasize that laments do contain complaints.[3] If the thought of airing your complaints to God makes you uncomfortable, you are not alone. In my Christian upbringing, I was taught the Bible's instructions that Christians should "give thanks in all circumstances" (1 Thessalonians 5:18) and do "all things without grumbling" (Philippians 2:14). Those things are true. But what I was taught with regard to them was not. Those verses cannot imply that we can never say anything negative to God or that doing so signals disobedience and discontentment. After all, more than fifty Psalms are songs of lament. And when you read them, you'll quickly notice they sound a lot like complaining in places. Scripture doesn't contradict itself, so how are we to reconcile these passages that seem to contradict one another?

The answer is that the lament is not just an airing of grievances; instead, it's a faithful type of prayer that voices the tension between our pain and God's goodness.[4] Lamenting allows God's people to share their grievances and gratitude at the same time.

The honest expression of your difficulties and pain even as you still pursue God has the benefit of helping to point the watching world to the Lord. Mere silence will not help others (or you) to press closer God. Pretending that your suffering isn't real or that it doesn't hurt will not help your spiritual walk or help others consider that Jesus just might be the hope they need. Without the contrasting backdrop of pain, the hope that we believers have in Christ does not stand out.

A denial of God rooted in suffering, or turning from God because of affliction, by contrast, may push others away from God. This is what Paul warns us about in Philippians 2:14–15, the "do all things without grumbling" passage I mentioned above. The context in verses 15 and 16 helps us understand these instructions regarding complaint. This particular warning is not against making any complaints or any negative statements at all; it warns that grumbling before a watching and corrupt world is a misused opportunity. Think about it this way. Should my complaints essentially put God on trial before an unbelieving world, I am not honoring him. But when I cry out in lament to God, with a faithful desire to be nearer to him in spite of my hurt, that does honor God. One way to check yourself on this matter is to ask, "Am I complaining to the world about God? Or am I bringing my complaints to God?"

A central tenant of Kellemen's book, *God's Healing for Life's Losses*, is that "It is normal to hurt and necessary to grieve."[5] The first time I read those words, however, I wrestled with them. My initial response was, "I don't need to grieve. I can just deal with hurts and move on. Kellemen, prove that I *have* to grieve."

At that time, I was getting counseling during a very difficult period in my life. My counselor asked me to list as much of the suffering I'd been through as I could remember. I mentioned that I had been sexually abused as a young child. But since we were meeting decades after that had taken place, I wasn't initially convinced that my past abuse had anything to do with my current difficulties. As our time together unfolded, though, I learned that I did need to grieve what had happened to me. I needed to grieve the ways it had impacted my life.

In the years since, I have noticed that PTS often results from not lamenting and grieving the losses we've experienced in life. When we don't grieve properly, the hurts don't go away. Instead, they get buried down inside us. We bury them with busyness, distraction, self-medication, or sheer willpower. But if you are struggling with PTS, you are acutely aware of what happens when loss isn't addressed the way

God intends. Despite our best efforts, those losses come back to haunt us in a myriad of ways.

For many who have been diagnosed with PTSD as adults, the trauma began far before the current crisis they are living through. Many who experience PTS as adults lived through traumatic events as children. For many reasons, they did not process that pain, and at some point it resurfaced.

God invites you to take your suffering, whether related to the distant past or some more recent hurt, to him. You can do this through prayer or journaling, with a friend or on your own. But don't delay. Begin talking to God about what is happening in your heart. All of it.

As you practice lament, remember that you belong to a loving God who doesn't expect you to gloss over suffering. He invites you to communicate with him about your difficulties. Scripture is full of examples of godly people doing the same. There is an entire book in the Bible called Lamentations. The Lord welcomes us to grieve in his presence and honestly express the pain we experience as a result of living in a fallen world.[6]

I encourage you to make some time to read Psalm 88. It is the darkest psalm in the Bible. Moreover, it doesn't have that characteristic U-turn found in many Psalms in which the psalmist goes down into the despair of suffering, only to find his way back to praise by the end. Psalm 88 starts in the pit, stays in the pit, and ends in the pit. Nevertheless, I find the chapter incredibly encouraging. Why? Because all throughout the psalm, a sufferer talks openly to God. He hasn't abandoned faith. He hasn't given up on his heavenly Father. Rather, in his pain he cries out to God with all that is in his heart. That is a beautiful way to handle suffering. That is lament.

I recommend that you talk to your counselor about this grief process called lamenting and how it applies to you. But even now, since you have come to this book because your life has been disoriented by trauma and you have losses in your life, take a few moments to just lift those losses to the Lord. Go to him and share your hurts. Ask your questions, and weep in his presence. He cares for you.

Keep in mind the way you approach God in prayer and lament is not going to be perfect. To demand that of weary and heavy-laden souls is unloving and that's never God's way. God invites you, his child, to draw near. He inclines himself toward you, not because you approach him in just the right way, but out of a deep love for you. So don't try to clean yourself up before you go into his presence—just go. Don't think you have to approach him with some theologically informed, holy language; speak what is on your heart the way you normally speak. A loving parent doesn't dismiss his small child just because his language is underdeveloped or he's yet to fully mature.

Another significant aspect of grieving is to invite others into the process. God has provided us with brothers and sisters in his church who can help us grieve. The Bible says, "Weep with those who weep" (Romans 12:15). You were not intended to suffer alone. God has commanded his people to come alongside you and compassionately weep with you. So please allow at least one or two to do this with you and for you. Part of what your Transformation Team can provide is compassion. Inviting them into your grief over the losses you have experienced can bless them tremendously. If you think about the last time you were able to help someone who was hurting, you'll likely agree that it was an honor—not an annoyance.

LETTING OTHERS LAMENT

"Hurting people hurt people" is a phrase commonly used among counselors and those who work in caring and helping fields. So how about it? Have you ever hurt anyone during your own pain? Perhaps you lashed out in anger at your children or your spouse or pushed away well-meaning family and friends who just wanted to help you. If so, did new trauma come about as a result of choices you made? Is it possible those choices hurt others, not just you?

I know that's a difficult paragraph to consider. You may feel like throwing this book across the room or into the trash now, but don't. I'm not here to pour salt into your wounds with these questions. I want to offer healing balm.

It's important that even as you learn to lament your own losses, you allow the people in your life to grieve the losses they have experienced. This can be hard for many reasons. For one, you might not think they need to grieve because your suffering seems so much worse than theirs. Or maybe it's tough because hearing about the hurt you've inflicted makes your cumulative pain feel too heavy to bear. Accepting responsibility for their pain may even seem unwise. But you need to accept a tough truth here: people who are close to those who've been disoriented by trauma suffer too.

Even if you haven't hurt your spouse, child, parent, or even a close friend directly, and even if they weren't present for the trauma you experienced, your losses are their losses as well. They hurt with you because they love you. And in some ways or circumstances, they have lost their dreams of the future they planned to share with you because of the changes that have taken place in you.

If as you read this, you realize you have directly hurt someone, don't deny or downplay their pain. After all, you know how hard it is when others do that to you. Instead, confess any sin you are aware of and seek forgiveness and reconciliation. Then encourage them to express the hurt they feel to someone who can help bear their burdens and point them to Christ. Make sure they know that as they do this, they are not gossiping, but grieving. Also, encourage them to take their concerns and hurts to God, who cares for them far better than you or any other person could.

Sometimes people disoriented by trauma feel guilt and shame over their experiences. And at times these feelings are entirely appropriate. Sometimes, after all, the trauma we experience is a consequence of foolish or sinful actions on our own part. But while it is quite common for people to believe they cannot (or should not) grieve losses that were brought about by their own wrong choices, God's Word directs us differently.

Whether losses were caused by your own sin, someone else's sin, or just in the course of living in a fallen world, almost all losses are worthy of grief. Don't believe that because your loss is not as bad as someone else's or because it came as a result of your own choices that it doesn't matter to God. He doesn't sit up in heaven saying, "Only come to me with the problems inflicted upon you. Those you caused, you'll have to deal with on your own." Nor does he say, "You got yourself into this mess, you get yourself out." Instead, he says in effect, "Bring all your cares to me because I care about you" (1 Peter 5:7).

In the next chapter I will discuss how God will help you deal with any shame and guilt stemming from the trauma you've experienced.

QUESTIONS FOR REFLECTION, DISCUSSION, & ACTION:

1. Describe your past grieving process. Based on what you've read in this chapter, what about it will need to change going forward?

2. What significant losses have you experienced in your life? Make a list of them and share it with your biblical counselor or mentor. Ask for his or her help in beginning to grieve those losses in a biblical way.

3. What is the biggest difference between lament and mere complaining?

Chapter 6

TAKE RESPONSIBILITY FOR WHAT YOU CAN

"I feel so guilty about what happened," Carl wept as he shared the account of his car accident. Although he had been cleared of all wrongdoing, he still wondered whether he was ultimately at fault for the death of the child in the other car. He also felt guilty because how he responded to his trauma has caused suffering for his own family. Sergeant Sanchez felt guilty too: for surviving the IED blast that killed Jake, for surviving a war that took the lives of so many of his fellow soldiers, and for killing enemy soldiers in Iraq and Afghanistan.

So how about you? Do you feel guilty over the experiences related to your trauma? Do you feel guilty about how you have responded to your trauma? Guilt often plagues trauma survivors, and ignoring guilty feelings does not make them go away. Instead, ignoring them will keep you from stepping into the hope and healing that God provides for those who struggle with guilt and shame.

If you are like most people disoriented by trauma, you are probably wrestling with some level of these things. Perhaps you feel responsible for your suffering. Maybe you think that if you made a different decision, your friends would still be alive. Maybe you think that if you had worn different clothes that day, he wouldn't have raped you. Such thoughts can be deeply distressing and extremely complicated. Processing such questions is an important step in your reorientation, but these are not topics you should try to process on your own. Throughout this book, I've recommended that you address your trauma with help from others. But this is one part of the journey you absolutely do not want to do alone. For one, because of your closeness to the experience, it will be hard for you to address these issues objectively.

Before we delve into how to assess your situation and deal with any guilt, it is important to define a few terms. Guilt and shame are two that are often used, but in many different ways. In this book, I use *guilt* to refer to the objective state of having done something sinful. That is similar to the legal use of the term: you are either guilty or not guilty. You either did something wrong or you didn't.

Shame is harder to define because it involves a number of complex human experiences. Often shame is the feeling associated with guilt. The latter is accompanied by negative feelings called shame. But shame can also exist when personal guilt is absent. Sometimes we feel shame because we think we have done something wrong, even when we haven't. We think we are guilty, so we feel shame even though we haven't done anything wrong. In his excellent book *Shame Interrupted*, Ed Welch defines *shame* this way: "Shame is the deep sense that you are unacceptable because of something you did, something done to you, or something associated with you. You feel exposed and humiliated."[1]

This covers a lot of territory. It means we can feel shame when we have done something wrong, but we also feel shame when others have wronged us. Victims of abuse, especially sexual abuse, feel this kind of shame acutely. In 2 Samuel 13, for instance, we read about the experience of Tamar, one of

King David's daughters. When it becomes clear that her half-brother intends to rape her, she asks, "As for me, where could I carry my shame?" (2 Samuel 13:13).

Shame is also something we feel when we step out of what our families or culture expects, or thinks is right. Whether it is sinful or not, when we are at odds with what society and the people around us believe is acceptable, we will feel the shame of being unacceptable, disgraced, and an outsider.

For those disoriented by trauma, issues of guilt and shame have to be addressed before a sufferer can become reoriented. Let's begin, then, with how to deal with the guilt you feel when you have done something wrong. Then we will address how to move forward from lingering feelings of shame and unworthiness.

DEALING WITH GUILT

If you have done something wrong (what the Bible calls sin), God has a wonderful, grace-filled solution. After coming to Jesus as your Savior, which is the only solution to your sin problem, you are called to live in ongoing repentance (1 John 1:8–10). This includes confessing what you did wrong, embracing God's forgiveness, providing restitution (if necessary), and reconciling with the person(s) you have wronged (when possible).

Being repentant means you have a change of heart about what you did that results in a change of behavior. Reaching a point of repentance usually follows first allowing ourselves to feel a measure of shame. It clues us in to the objective reality that we did something wrong. This can motivate us to alter our beliefs, desires, and feelings that led to the behavior so that in the future we behave differently. If you stole something from a store, you should feel shame. And that sense of shame should motivate you to turn from wanting something so much you would steal to get it.

Yet to repent takes things a step further. It requires confession. *Confession* is honestly acknowledging your sin to God and to those you have sinned against. Halfhearted apologies, making excuses, and twisting your story to something other than the truth are all ways to avoid and undermine true confession. If you are not honest with God and others about your sin, true confession has not taken place.

The next step in addressing personal sin is seeking forgiveness. When you have sinned against someone, part of repentance is asking for forgiveness from God and the person you wronged. You can read King David's plea for God to forgive him in Psalm 51. There he confesses the sin of assaulting Bathsheba and killing her husband to cover up what he did. David asks for mercy and grace directly from God. Asking for forgiveness should always start with going to God, since all sin is ultimately against him. Then we can go to the person we have harmed and ask him or her to forgive us too.

The next step in repentance is making restitution. In short, that means to restore. If, for example, something was stolen, restitution means ensuring that what was taken gets returned. Sometimes it involves an additional payment beyond what was stolen. To see this principle in action, check out the story of Zacchaeus in Luke 19:1–10. Restoration, though, is not possible in all circumstances. Some things cannot be undone. Attempts can be made to undo damage caused by gossip or slander by going to those who heard it and setting the record straight, but even that does not guarantee the full restoration of one's reputation.

Reconciling is the final step in the solution for guilt caused by sin. This is the act of moving forward in the relationship that sin harmed. Not every relationship will move forward to the same status that it enjoyed before hurt entered it, however. A wife whose husband abandons her, divorces her, and remarries someone else will not be able to maintain the same kind of relationship she had with her ex before—not even if he repents and asks for forgiveness. Nevertheless, many relationships can continue and move forward.

Where trauma is concerned, however, finding forgiveness from an injured party becomes more complex. The opportunity to address sin and seek forgiveness may not be possible or advisable. Sins committed on the battlefield, for instance, typically cannot be revisited. And if you are the perpetrator of sin leading to trauma, including your own, you may never get to seek forgiveness from the people you sinned against. In all such instances, you can rest in the forgiveness available from God.

I must point out that there are times when shame persists even when one has addressed objective guilt. The way forward in those instances is to ask God to help you view yourself the way he does. Committing certain passages of Scripture to memory will prove helpful. Also, ask your Transformation Team to remind you about the forgiveness you have in Jesus Christ and what the Bible says about all who put their faith in him. Below are a few examples. I've cast them as "I am" statements to help you take them to heart.

- I am of great value and share the same heavenly Father with Jesus (Matthew 6:26; Romans 8:15).
- I am one whose sins are remembered no more (Hebrews 8:12).
- I am one set free from slavery to sin, an heir of God (Galatians 4:7).
- I am one chosen to be blameless and holy and was predestined to be adopted into God's family (Ephesians 1:4–6).
- I am Christ's friend (Luke 12:4).

I've provided a list of more of these statements for you in Resource 4. I encourage you to regularly review them, meditate on them, and thank God for his forgiveness and love.

It must be acknowledged that remembering your sin does not necessarily have to lead to you experiencing more shame. There is a healthy, biblical way of remembering your sin. King David, for instance, wrote two beautiful psalms describing the way God graciously dealt with his terrible sins of sexual abuse and murder (Psalms 32 and 51). In Psalm 51:3 David writes, "I know my transgressions, and my sin is ever before me." Nevertheless, in Psalm 32:1, 5 he says, "Blessed is the one whose transgression is forgiven. . . . [Y]ou [God] forgave the iniquity of my sin." Since we have experienced the loving, gracious forgiveness of God like David, we too can reflect on our sins in ways that can fill our hearts with thankfulness because of what God has delivered us from and forgiven us for. However when we focus on the awful nature of what we did instead of the victory of Christ over our sin, it will foster shame. It will make us feel separated from God.

DEALING WITH SHAME THAT DOESN'T STEM FROM GUILT

Carl felt shame over the death of the child in the accident he was involved in, even though he was not at fault. Sergeant Sanchez felt shame for surviving in combat, while others did not—an experience often called *survivor's guilt.* It's helpful to know that when properly understood, shame often resolves as someone sorts through genuine guilt versus confused guilt and then deals with guilt in the biblical way described above.[2] However, especially in trauma, there are many occasions in which people feel shame or a sense of guilt when they weren't guilty of doing anything wrong.

When we feel shame and there is no objective guilt, our goal (again) should be to see ourselves as God sees us. If you are a Christian, someone who has put your faith in the saving work of Jesus, then God declares you to be clean and holy. Thanks to what Jesus accomplished and your trust in him, everything that was shameful about you has been washed away. God the Father sees you as pure.

Also helpful on this topic is realizing that Jesus drew near to people cut off by shame. He touched lepers who, because of their skin disease, had to live outside the city. They had to cry, "Unclean!" to keep anyone from accidentally touching them or approaching (Matthew 8:1–4). Jesus often drew near to those who were cut off from society because of disease, defilement, or poor decisions (Mark 5:1–20; Luke 7:36–38; John 4:1–30). It seems that every time Jesus touched them, his cleanness and purity was transferred to them.

The amazing transfer of our shame to Jesus happened on the cross when Jesus took on all the guilt and the shame of his people (Isaiah 53:4–11; 1 Peter 2:24). When we trust in him to cleanse us from our sins, the credit for his perfect goodness is given to us (Romans 4:1–5; 2 Corinthians 5:21). Our shame is washed away because we are no longer unclean from our own sin, the sin done to us, or any other judgment from others. God sees us as his perfect, holy, lovable children. And he wants us to get to know him better and stay near.

When you rest in the loving acceptance and care of God the Father, your shame will begin to fade away. As you realize how much his opinion of you matters, it overshadows any thought of what other people think of you. Even if someone else has judged you as wanting and unworthy of honor, you'll begin to realize you do not have to take on that shame. What God believes about you is paramount, so anyone else's contrary opinion can fall away as you draw closer to him.

Think back to what Carl and Sergeant Sanchez went through. Would you say that either of them was guilty of sinning in the matter of what happened? Would you look at those men whom Jesus forgave with disgust and shame? Or would you encourage them to turn to God, let go of any feelings of shame, and believe what God says about them? I have no doubt you would encourage them. So will you also encourage yourself with the same truths about God's love and acceptance?

SORTING IT OUT

One thing that many find challenging is determining whether they are legitimately guilty or not. The following chart is meant to help you address any confusion you might feel. It is adapted from a helpful tool in pastor Steve Viars's book, *Putting Your Past in Its Place: Moving Forward in Freedom and Forgiveness*.[3] Viars describes four "buckets," or places, in which you may find yourself related to your trauma or events connected to it. Start by thinking about which of the four numbered boxes best represents where you are with relation to a specific event.

		In What Occurred, You Were	
		Innocent	Guilty
Your response	You responded in a godly way	1. Christlike suffering	3. Remembering the forgiveness of sin with thanksgiving
	You responded in a sinful way	2. Humble analysis	4. Honest self-confrontation

Box 1, "Christlike suffering," describes a situation in which you were innocent in whatever took place, and you responded to your situation in a godly way. For instance,

Sergeant Javier Sanchez was not responsible or guilty for the IED explosion that killed Jake. If Javier responded to his suffering with lament and biblical grief, then he is innocent in his response as well.

It is, however, still possible for people to wrestle with difficulties, especially shame, even if they experience Christlike suffering. Sergeant Sanchez could be wrestling with survivor's guilt. Someone helping him needs to point out the truth that he is not guilty, he committed no sin, and in no way caused or could have prevented Jake's death. He also needs to learn how to turn to God in a biblical lament. The painful feelings he is dealing with, which drive him to take responsibility for Jake dying, or to see his own survival as somehow wrong could be tied to legitimate sorrow over the loss of his friend. Processing grief God's way is how to handle those painful feelings.

It could be, though, that Sergeant Sanchez is stuck in Box 2, "Humble analysis" if, while innocent of any wrongdoing that led to Jake's death, he has responded sinfully to the stress of trauma he experienced. If Javier turned to substance abuse to mask or numb his pain, or lashed out at those around him, he is not dealing with his suffering in a Christlike way.

This next idea may be hard for you to hear. If you are dealing with your suffering with negative behavior, remember that it's a kindness for your Transformation Team to raise these issues with you. The fact that significant suffering has entered your life and that your responses are common and "understandable" does not take away the fact that they are wrong and hurtful to you and others. The only way to truly handle sin is the process outlined above. Acknowledging a lack of guilt leading up to the trauma, but also admitting the reality of the wrongness of the sinful responses, is the only way to loosen their grip on your life.

Something else bothering Sergeant Sanchez has to do with the killing he did in combat. Many civilians are quick to dismiss the shame and feelings of guilt associated with that. They often say things like, "You didn't do anything wrong. You were just doing your job," or, "Killing in combat is different from murder. God doesn't condemn killing for your country or to protect life. Thank you for your service." While those statements contain some truth (and possibly truth the veteran needs to hear), they are often offered too quickly. Those saying them rarely take the time to hear what is truly bothering the veteran.

If words like these are shared too early, it may actually heap more shame on a person, causing them to clam up even tighter than before. Why? Because what some people who've killed in combat are afraid to admit is that they really enjoyed taking out bad guys. Whether they were motivated by a desire for revenge, or some other sinfully motivated delight in killing, the pleasure they felt now haunts them. This is often what is behind thinking of oneself as a monster, or claiming, "If people really knew me they would run away from me and have me locked up." This paragraph gets at the way Sergeant Sanchez felt about the killing he did in combat.

The Bible is not ignorant of or silent about this issue. In 1 Samuel 25:28–31, Abigail stands up to King David in defense of her servants and confronts the sinful motivation driving his murderous plot to annihilate her husband and household. Importantly, she doesn't critique David for killing in combat. He, like many other godly men in the Old Testament, is a warrior. She even praises his military exploits. But she does warn him that killing for his own name's sake, or out of vengeance, could cause "grief or pangs of conscience for having shed blood without cause or . . . working salvation himself" (1 Samuel 25:31). King David confirms her theory as preserving him from incurring serious guilt when he responds this way: "[B]lessed be you, who have kept me this day from bloodguilt . . . !" (1 Samuel 25:33).

If David had gone ahead with his plan to take revenge on Nabal and all the innocent men in his household out of selfish motives, he would have been guilty. That would have led to him being haunted by the accompanying shame. Javier Sanchez admits that he did go on to kill out of vengeance and hatred after Jake died. And now, like a living illustration of what Abigail warned about, he is haunted with overwhelming shame. He fears what would happen should his wife or children find out what a monster he was. What would they think of him if they knew he had delighted in killing? Javier is therefore squarely in Box 4 of the above chart in relation to this issue. He sinned by killing in vengeful hate, and so far he has only pursued sinful means of covering his guilt and shame. But what he needs is to approach God in humble confession of his sin, ask God's forgiveness, and accept God's promise that he forgives and washes away the shame from "*ALL* unrighteousness" (1 John 1:9, emphasis added). It is not always necessary, but it can be a helpful step to talk through this with a biblical counselor, pastor, or other spiritual mentor. Such persons can help someone process what they have done, while also affirming God's love, grace, mercy, and forgiveness for those who repent.

There may be no way to reconcile or make restitution in this kind of case. But reconciliation with God is always possible. Someone who trusts in the atoning death and resurrection of Jesus has received forgiveness and cleansing from all his sin and is now a child of God. Going to God with the specific sins and shame we deal with, whether linked to events pre-salvation or after, is a way of reminding ourselves of the forgiveness he freely gives. Doing that moves us from

Box 4 to Box 3: "Remembering the forgiveness of sins with thanksgiving." When we look back toward our sin and realize the cross of Jesus and the forgiveness he won are standing between us and it, our hearts should overflow with gratitude. And as they do, we tend to stop thinking about our sin so we can marvel at Christ's power to conquer sin and death, and to realize that he really has given us eternal life (1 Corinthians 15:54–57).

As you walk through various incidents in your life with your counselor, work with him or her to identify which box you are in, in relation to each situation. One beauty of the gospel is that God provides solutions for you, no matter where you are.

DON'T TAKE RESPONSIBILITY WHEN YOU CAN'T

One of the saddest situations I see as a counselor involves individuals accepting responsibility for sins that were committed against them. Even sadder are those times when I see people burdened because others have heaped condemnation on them for sins they themselves did not commit. This is what is commonly and accurately called *victim shaming*.

Let me say this clearly. Up to this point I've largely avoided examples of sexual assault because I know they can be particularly distressing to people who have lived through similar things. If that is a trigger for you, please stop reading and skip ahead to the next section.

No matter what someone might have done or not done, she or he is not responsible for being sexually assaulted. The assailant is completely responsible. Even if the injured party made unwise or even wrong choices, those do not justify assault. Nor do they transfer any responsibility from the criminal to the victim.

When you are sorting through hurts in your life, take responsibility for sins that you commit. But don't take on the sins of others or blame yourself for accidents or other things outside your control.

WHAT DOES FORGIVENESS LOOK LIKE IF YOU HAVE BEEN TERRIBLY HARMED?

What do you do when your trauma is the direct result of someone's sin against you? One of the greatest examples of what biblical forgiveness looks and sounds like in a situation like that comes from the victim statement given by Rachael Denhollander at the trial of Larry Nasser.[4] The latter was convicted of sexually assaulting female gymnasts who were under his care as doctor for the USA Gymnastics team. Rachael was the last of 156 victims to give a statement. In hers, Rachael does something surprising and profound: she offers forgiveness to Nasser. But she does so on condition: he first needs to repent of his sin. Note that she does not grant him forgiveness, but she is *prepared to* forgive him *if* he repents and asks for it.

Rachael has already gone to God with the sin committed against her. Doing that is often called *attitudinal forgiveness*. It means she laid the sin against her before God, set aside bitterness and claims for personal vengeance, and in one sense has forgiven Nasser from the heart. This is the vertical element of forgiveness—we forgive others in our hearts before God. This is the first step in forgiveness. Now, if there is repentance from Nasser and also a request for forgiveness, Rachael is ready to offer *transactional forgiveness* too—that's the horizontal element of offering forgiveness to another person.[5] Vertical forgiveness before God is always possible and always healing. But horizontal forgiveness—in which you give total forgiveness to the one who harmed you—is not always possible or wise.

How to handle forgiveness for sins against you that resulted in trauma can be a complex issue. That's why I urge you to walk through the question with a biblical counselor or other spiritual mentor. The two of you could read through the book *Making Sense of Forgiveness: Moving from Hurt toward Hope*, by Brad Hambrick. As you go, you can discuss which principles apply to your particular situation.

Here are two general ones:

1. Forgiving does not mean all consequences disappear. It does not take away legal culpability and legal implications. It also doesn't require everyone to go back to the way things were. For instance, even if Larry Nasser did repent and ask forgiveness of every one of his victims and all forgave him, he should remain behind bars so that legal justice gets served. If someone has abused you, forgiveness will not require you to reengage in that relationship. Nor will it keep you from putting guardrails in place to prevent future abuse.
2. As Rachael's brave testimony demonstrates, forgiveness is possible, even for those who commit the most heinous sins. And it is possible for victims of heinous sin to forgive from the heart. Holding onto bitterness, hatred, and vengeance, however, will do harm to your soul.

WHAT ABOUT SO-CALLED GRAY AREAS?

You have probably noticed that personal guilt and innocence are not always easily determined. Perhaps you don't remember all the details accurately. Your actions may have been "legal," but you could be struggling with guilt because you are unsure of your motives. There are lots of reasons why some answers remain hazy and difficult to sort out. In the end, you and your counselor may not be able to parse out every detail and determine exactly how much you are responsible for. But the beauty of the gospel is that you don't have to. As much value as there is in having answers, and as helpful as it can be to discern the truth of what happened in each situation, all guilt—for those who love Jesus—is covered by his blood. Even if there are parts of your story that you are responsible for and you don't recognize it, your guilt is covered and you can rest in the forgiveness offered to you by Christ.

The Bible explains that you were once so deeply in debt to God that there was no way you could ever pay off your debt. Worse, dealing with sin (including your own) required the sacrifice of a completely innocent human being—which no one can claim to be (Romans 3:23; Hebrews 9:22). But the good news is that God took on human form in the person of Jesus (Hebrews 1:3). Jesus lived a perfect life, then willingly laid it down so that his shed blood could pay for all the sins of those who trust in his sacrifice (Romans 5:6–11; Hebrews 9:13–14).

The promises of the gospel are offered freely by God to anyone who turns to him in repentance and faith, trusting in Jesus in the sense I've just described. God promises that all who call out to him will be forgiven (Romans 10:8–13). There is no restitution for you to make because Jesus already paid your debt through what he did on the cross (Ephesians 2:8–9; Titus 3:5). You move toward him and become more and more like him as you read about him in Scripture and obey what he says.

QUESTIONS FOR REFLECTION, DISCUSSION, & ACTION:

1. How prominent of a role does wrestling with guilt and shame have in your life? Are you experiencing shame that does not stem from true guilt? If so, explain.

2. How should the gospel and what God says about you impact your view of self? How can it positively address your feelings of shame?

Chapter 7
BUILDING RESILIENCY

If you've ever spent much time around forests, you know that trees respond differently to storms. Some varieties, like oaks, have solid sturdy trunks that don't bend with the wind; they resist it. These are seemingly unmoved and undisturbed by storms. Other trees, like palms, bend with the wind, gently righting themselves once the wind eases. Still other types, like the coastal cypress trees that line parts of the California coast, adapt their shape over time and with each storm that comes. These trees end up looking as though they are bending to the wind even when there is no breeze present. I bring this up because each type of tree I've mentioned represents one of the three primary ways used to describe resiliency or people who are resilient.[1]

WHICH GROUP ARE YOU CURRENTLY IN?

Resilient Like the Oak Tree

Some people seem unmoved or unbothered by suffering when it hits. These people are represented by the oak tree. They appear to be strong and tough, beyond impact by the suffering around them. Though storms of suffering rage, they remain unaffected.

Resilient Like the Palm Tree

Other people are obviously affected by suffering, but they seem to bounce back to just the way they were before the storms came. They seem to deal with no lasting effects from the suffering they experience.

Resilient Like the Coastal Cypress Tree

Still other people are shaped by the suffering they experience. They don't appear unmoved, nor do they bounce back into place when the storm passes. Instead, they adapt. Each time, they take on a new shape—one that is better equipped to handle the next storm that passes.

Each of these approaches to suffering has strengths and weaknesses. Many tend to think that it is always great to be like the oak tree—unmoved by the traumatic experiences one lives through. And it could be that you are hoping that although suffering has bent you down, you can learn to rebound like the palm tree in every instance. But I believe that God's way for us to deal with the storms of life is to be more like the coastal cypress, the tree that bends with each storm and takes on new form.

PURPOSEFUL WORK IN PROGRESS

In this chapter, it will prove beneficial to keep in mind that when you were born again into God's family, you were already a beautiful work of art—but you still aren't a finished one. And I'm not either. God, our Creator, is like a master sculptor who works at shaping every one of his children until the time comes for them to see his face. But while this might at first seem disheartening, the Bible teaches us that God is at work molding and shaping each of us into something wonderful: a reflection of Jesus (Romans 8:28–30). To accomplish that, he uses everything that comes into our lives as a tool: people and places, delights and doldrums, temptations and trials. Like coastal winds and storms, the circumstances of life push you, bend you, and reshape you. Sometimes the bending hurts, but it does not have to break you (2 Corinthians 4:8–9). Rather, it can help you be better able to handle the storms of life to come.

Like a master sculptor busily chipping away at the marble slab he intends to become a masterpiece, God also is eyeing a model as he works on us. Did you catch his name in that previous paragraph? He is the perfect image of what humans can and should be and his name is Jesus. From the time you put your faith in him, everything that happens is a tool in the hand of a Master who wants to make you more like Jesus. Your traumatic experiences are no exception.

In the following chapters we will talk about some of the many ways in which God can use your trauma in the way I'm talking about. It is not a painless process, but it is a powerful one, and one for your ultimate good. As you become more like Jesus, you'll become the best version of yourself. And that means you will better reflect God to the world—shining the light of his love to those around you. This is the ultimate purpose for which you were created, and it outshines any other. This is a purpose that can stay with you all throughout your life here.

Precisely how this happens and what it looks like is unique to each believer, but don't miss the answer to one of life's ultimate questions. People are created to shine with God's love and to glorify him. I know the idea of being created to bring God glory can sound abstract, so let me make it more concrete for you. Think about the most breathtakingly beautiful place you have been: the Grand Canyon, the Alps, the Amalfi Coast, Everest, and Yosemite National Park might be great contenders. Once that's in mind, think about what happens when you visit those places and experience their beauty. You can't help but feel amazed, inspired, and in awe! You long to stay there, to explore, to find more hidden gems of beauty. Your thoughts are filled with praises for that place. When you leave, you might wonder how you could share that experience with another. That will lead you to realize you can tell others about it and that will probably spark some interest in their hearts too. When you get home, you show them pictures. You hope that will evoke some discussion and their longing to visit. Nevertheless, you know nothing can compare to the moment in which each friend you share with first encounters the place for themselves. That is much what glorifying God is like. And the more we glorify him, the more others' hearts tend to be inclined toward him.

Enduring trauma and suffering can seem like a long journey to nowhere. Life can feel meaningless, and every day like a struggle. But God has given you a purpose, one particularly great reason to get up in the morning and to keep going through each day he provides you. That purpose is to glorify him (Isaiah 43:6–7; 1 Corinthians 10:31; 2 Corinthians 5:9).

You and I bring glory to God by reflecting his character to others, by sharing his love, and by proclaiming the amazing gift of forgiveness for sins and life eternal that Jesus offers. The very best way to show people what God is like is by becoming more and more like Jesus through trusting obedience, while we grow in love for God and for people.

God promises that everything that happens in life is geared toward that end for everyone who follows him. The apostle Paul writes,

> And we know that for those who love God all things work together for good, for those who are called according to his purpose. For those whom he foreknew he also predestined to be conformed to the image of his Son, in order that he might be the firstborn among many brothers. (Romans 8:28–29)

Perhaps this is a passage of the Bible that has already been shared with you in an unhelpful way. Many well-meaning Christians turn to verse 28 *anytime* someone faces *any kind* of trial. With it they hope to alleviate suffering quickly by reminding others that God has a good plan that is at work through the suffering. This is ultimately true, and we'll return to it in the next chapter, but often such blanket use of Scripture is off base in two primary ways.

First, it tends to lack compassion. Christ cares about you and your suffering in a personalized way—not a general one. While you are experiencing the disorientation of trauma, just being reminded that God is up to good can sound trite, simplistic, and uncaring—like receiving a pat on the back and an empty promise that it will all be okay. That turns a profound biblical promise into a mere platitude and robs people of the real hope that is contained in these words. People need time to grieve the losses they experience in life before being rushed along to the promises of future good. That is why I earlier urged the practice of biblical lament. The healing process begins with acknowledging and grieving the real hurts you have been through. We need to go to God with our sorrows before we start trying to identify what good he might possibly bring out of them—such as the coastal cypress shaping that he may accomplish through them.

The second way a blanket use of this Romans 8 passage can be harmful is that those offering it may misrepresent the "good" that is promised. Imagine, for example, telling the person whose fiancé just dumped her, "Don't worry, God works all things for your good. Surely he has a better spouse for you in the future." While God might orchestrate a broken engagement to prevent one marriage and pave the way for another, that is not what is promised in this passage of Scripture. The passage is very clear, but we need to change our focus from the word "good" to the word "for" that appears at the beginning of verse 29 to see it. What God promises is that he will use everything that happens in life (the good and the bad) to work good *for* those who love him and are called according to his purposes. And that "good" is explained in verse 29. God uses everything "to [conform us] to the image of his Son."

So God promises that everything that comes into your life can, thanks to him, help to make you more like Jesus, so that you will better reflect him to the watching world. And as you do, you'll be living out the purpose of bringing glory to him.

What does this discussion have to do with resiliency and reorienting life after trauma? Remember the trees. When pain comes into your life, including the intense suffering associated with trauma, God's plan is not that you be unchanged by it. He wants you to press close to him and to allow him to work though *all things* to transform you to become more like Jesus.

Hang on to these truths for dear life. You exist for a reason. Your life has purpose. Your purpose may not be what you once thought it was, and that can be a hard reality to accept. But losing what you thought was your purpose may well be part of God's plan to help you live in light of your better, higher purpose—one that will fill your life with meaning, significance, honor, and joy.

The answer to life's big question, "Why do I exist?" is answered by God: "You exist to glorify me." How might this foundational truth influence the way you experience your past? This is the question we will turn to in the next chapter.

QUESTIONS FOR REFLECTION, DISCUSSION, & ACTION:

1. Before you read this chapter, how would you have defined your purpose in life? What, if anything, has changed with regard to that topic?

2. How does the idea that God can use even the toughest things we go through to make us more like Jesus make you feel?

3. What hard things did Jesus go through during his lifetime on earth so that he could better identify with you?

PART 3

Learning to Reorient Your Past, Present, and Future

Chapter 8
REORIENTING YOUR PAST

As you know from firsthand experience with PTS, one's past can regularly invade the present. And it can dominate one's whole life. But something that will help put the past in its place is reorienting how we view the past to align with God's view. This may include altering long-held beliefs about God, your family, people in general, or yourself. In the counseling I do, I regularly ask people to consider the various functions of their hearts (thoughts, will, and emotions) as they apply to the primary relationships of life (God, others, self, and circumstances) with relation to a past traumatic event. Then I ask them to use an empty version of the chart below to help sort out all that was happening in themselves and in their relationships during that event.[1]

When, for instance, Sergeant Javier Sanchez reflected on an IED attack that killed his best friend and led to his own medical discharge from the Army, his responses looked like this:

	Thoughts/ Beliefs (Cognition)	Choices/ Desires (Volition)	Emotions (Affection)
God	Where was God? If there even is a God, why did he let this happen?	I wish God would have shown up that day and saved my friend.	I'm confused whether or not God exists. I'm frustrated that God didn't do anything.
Others	I think Jake should have lived. I hate the people who carried out the attack. Why didn't someone see the IED and avoid it?	I wish Jake had survived. I want to kill those responsible for his death.	I am extremely sad over losing Jake. I burn with rage toward those who killed him. I'm frustrated with the rest of the convoy for not avoiding the IED. I'm frustrated with the commanders who made us go on that pointless convoy.
Myself	I think I deserved to die more than Jake did.	I wish I had died instead of Jake, or at least with him.	I feel ashamed that I survived when so many others didn't.
Circum-stances	I don't understand why that happened. Why did our convoy have to get hit? Why were we there in the first place?	I wish it hadn't happened.	I'm sad about losing Jake and losing so many others. I'm angry that all that stuff happened, and I'm angry about being taken out of the fight.

What do you think about Javier's responses? Do they reflect any of your thoughts about your trauma? How, if at all, can you relate to what he says? I hope that this look into his replies will serve as a reminder of the truth we discussed at the beginning of the book: *You are not alone.*

You'll find several charts like this one in the back of this volume. Take a minute to turn to and fill out the one titled "My Past Past" on pages 122–23. As you do, write down the first thing that comes to mind in each of the categories as you reflect on your past. Then return to this section.

It's important to remember that while your past cannot be changed, it can be redeemed. Redeeming your past starts as you reorient your view to be oriented with God's view of your past.

When you look at your past and the events that traumatized you, what purpose do you see? Often one of the hardest things about our suffering is how pointless it seems. But God doesn't look at your past that way. He sees significance, meaning, and purpose in every aspect of your life. On this side of heaven, you are not likely to get answers to all the why questions you have related to your trauma. But in the Bible God does clearly reveal some reasons for our suffering.

OUR SUFFERING ACCOMPLISHES GOOD

As we began to discuss in the previous chapter, the first guaranteed purpose for your pain is that God can use it to accomplish the good of making you more like Jesus. Joni Eareckson Tada, a woman who became a quadriplegic after a diving accident at the age of seventeen, has a wise comment with relation to this point. She says, "Sometimes God allows what he hates to accomplish what he loves."[2] Indeed, although God hates suffering, he—amazingly—uses it to fulfill his purpose for our lives.

The Bible is full of stories that illustrate what I mean. One of the clearest examples is the story of Joseph that appears in Genesis 37 and Genesis 39–50. Joseph's life starts out great—he is one of his father's favorite sons among twelve. At a young age, he is given responsibility, a divinely provided dream of success, and great clothes. But his story quickly turns tragic as Joseph endures one traumatic event after an another:

- His brothers, who are jealous of him, plot his murder. But in the end, they sell him to slave traders instead. These cart him off to Egypt.
- As a slave, Joseph gets falsely accused of attempted rape and thrown into prison. For years.
- Though Joseph spends his incarceration helping and serving others, he is quickly forgotten by the prisoner whom he encourages the most. The one who gets returned to service at Pharoah's side and could help him out.

Two years go by before Joseph is called on to interpret Pharaoh's dream of famine coming to the land. Only then, by God's grace, is he elevated to being second in command of Egypt. God works through him to prepare for the coming famine, saving the lives of people in Egypt. But the careful reader of Scripture soon realizes that Joseph is given this opportunity in part to save the lives of his Israelite family, through whom the promised Savior of the world was destined to come.

Even after enjoying provision from their ill-treated sibling throughout the course of the famine, Joseph's brothers—who had since relocated to the land of his enslavement/rise to fame—feel sure that Joseph will exact vengeance on them immediately after their father dies. But here is what I want you to see. Joseph has a different perspective on the terrible events in his life that were kicked off by their sin against him. He says, "You meant evil against me, but God meant it for good, to bring it about that many people should be kept alive, as they are today" (Genesis 50:20). Joseph had man's perspective on his suffering; he was well aware of his brothers' intention—to do evil. Nevertheless, *he also chose to see God's intention*—to preserve his people and the line that would bring Jesus to save the world from sin and to one day to deliver it from all sorrow (Revelation 21:1–5).

Perhaps it's hard right now to imagine any such good purposes being accomplished in relation to your suffering. God, after all, often reveals them to us slowly and over many years. Some purposes he preserves for us to be revealed only in eternity. But keep your heart and eyes open for positive purposes. And when God shows you some new way in which he has worked good through your suffering, praise him for it.

Each year I live, I recognize new good with relation to my past trauma. Every time I notice a lesson I've learned as a result of it, encounter new people I'm able to help because of it, and see new ways I've become more like Jesus for having went through it, I'm encouraged to keep pressing forward. Taking notice of how God has been at work through my suffering fills me with gratitude for how he is able to take a terrible thing and somehow use it for good.

Pause and take some time to ask God to help you see his hand at work through the tough events of your past. Consider how you might come to see your past differently in light of the kind of grand plan revealed through Joseph's story. It may help to ask those on your Transformation Team to brainstorm with you about this. Try to see any good, even a tiny glimmer of good, that might already be unfolding with relation to the trauma you've experienced.

After Javier reconsidered his past in the way I'm advocating, he made a follow-up chart to his first one that looked like this:

	Thoughts/ Beliefs (Cognition)	Choices/ Desires (Volition)	Emotions (Affection)
God	God was there the day Jake died. God was with me. He preserved my life.	I wish God had saved Jake's life. I want to know more of his reasons for what happened.	I was certainly scared, and I grieve the loss of Jake and other losses that resulted from that explosion. But I am also thankful to know God is working through my pain.
Others	I am thankful to have known Jake and still think of him often. I don't know what to think about the people who set the explosives. I'm still working through that.	I wish Jake had survived. I would like justice to come to the people responsible and wish they would turn away from evil and know the true and living God.	I still grieve the loss of Jake. I feel something like pity for the people who killed him because they don't realize how wrong they are and the judgment that awaits them if they don't repent.
Myself	I know God has a purpose for keeping me here.	I want to live in a way that honors Jake's memory and honors God.	I feel thankful and joyful to be used by God to bless others.
Circum-stances	I don't understand every reason why our convoy was hit, but I know God was in control of it.	I still wish it hadn't happened, but I want to make it count by living a good life.	I'm still sad at the loss, but also thankful to have survived. I'm hopeful that I might somehow see a little good come out of those circumstances that led me to this place in life.

Take some time now and fill out the "My Reoriented Past" chart on page 125 with a perspective reoriented to God's. Then continue reading this chapter.

REORIENTING THE MEMORIES

"If I wanted to get rid of the memories, I'd have to get a lobotomy," said one man as he sat with a group of veterans discussing aspects of their experiences of PTS. Many people, like him, wish their bad memories would go away one way or another. Some pursue counseling with the expectation that they will. Others hope to find a pill that will make them forget. When such avenues don't bring the desired result, many turn to substance abuse to try to keep the memories at bay.

God does not want you to be overwhelmed by your bad memories, but he doesn't want you to forget them either. I've already laid the groundwork to help you avoid becoming overwhelmed by such memories when they come, and you've now got a Peace Plan and a general way to reorient your heart's view of the past. Now I want you, with the help of a counselor or trusted friend, to consider deeper truths regarding your memories. I've already pointed out the value of realizing that memories are in the past and not the present, that the things in memories cannot actually hurt us now, and that things in our memories are not likely to recur in our present contexts. But what are some deeper truths related to your specific memories that can help turn your mind away from overwhelming fear and toward worship and deeper appreciation for God?

I realize what I'm advocating may sound unrealistic, so let me show you an example. Whenever a traumatic memory includes the loss of life, we can reorient that memory by choosing to be thankful for that person we lost. We can be thankful for the life he or she lived and the opportunity we had to know them. We can be thankful for the experiences we enjoyed together. True, these thoughts may elicit sorrow and grief over our losses, but sorrow is not bad or wrong. In fact, as we saw in chapter 5, grief is God's way of helping us address the suffering and loss we experience. The greater the loss, the greater the sorrow. Did you know that when you weep over the loss of a dear loved one, it is an indication of how much he or she meant to you?

As we've discussed, Vanessa and Javier both lost people very dear to them. The memories of the events that took their loved ones away are extremely painful. Thinking of the good times they had with their loved ones who died could by itself provoke the memories of their deaths. Fear of doing just that often prevented them from remembering even the good times. That only added further misery for Javier and Vanessa because they felt as though they were abandoning or forgetting their loved ones as a result. As the two reoriented their hearts to see the way God sees, they realized they could reverse this cycle. Instead of allowing fear of the painful memories to keep them from reflecting on the good ones, they began to see even the painful memories as opportunities to remember the better times. By taking their thoughts captive and reorienting them to what is true, right, and good, they learned the memories did not have to spiral downward. Instead, they could direct their thoughts toward the pleasant memories and toward praising God. This practice enabled them to draw near to the one who gave them life. When no longer motivated by fear to isolate themselves, they were also encouraged to draw closer to their families and friends.

Adding thoughts of gratitude gives a different quality to your sorrow. In fact, this kind of sorrow is unique to Christians. We have the immense privilege of being able to look for the hand of God, our loving Father, at work throughout our lives—even in the hardest things.

Perhaps right now that perspective seems out of your reach. I encourage you, then, to start by asking God and others to help you reframe your past so that you stop assuming God is absent or uncaring but is instead intimately involved with you and is at work for your good, for the good of others, and for his glory despite allowing what he hates. When you can accept this, you'll find the past is significantly reoriented. It will be brought into alignment with what God wants for you while also propelling you forward. In the next chapter we will discuss how this can help you deal with your present life.

QUESTIONS FOR REFLECTION, DISCUSSION, & ACTION:

1. With a trusted friend or counselor, fill out the "My Past Past" chart on pages 122–23. To the best of your ability, list the things that were going on in your heart at the time of your traumatic experience.

2. With your trusted friend or counselor, list the primary beliefs, feelings, and desires you have toward God.

3. Consider whether the points on your list match up with what the Bible says about him. This may necessitate familiarizing yourself with passages about his character, like Numbers 23:19; Psalms 18:30; 116:5; Titus 1:2; 2 Peter 3:9; and 1 John 1:5; 4:8.

Chapter 9
REORIENTING YOUR PRESENT

Honk-honk-hooooonk! Several months ago, Carl's body shook as he was brought back to reality by that horn blaring from the vehicle behind him. Gasping for air, he forced himself to ease off the brake and release the steering wheel from the white-knuckled stranglehold he had on it. Unfortunately, it was not the first time that particular intense reaction to an everyday fact of traffic had happened. Ever since his accident, when Carl drove by a line of backed-up traffic, he struggled with PTS. His heart would race and sometimes images of a car darting out in front of him invaded his mind to the point he would slam on the brakes even though there wasn't a car in front of him. Those episodes left Carl feeling fearful, embarrassed, and ashamed. Sometimes he wondered if he would ever be able to drive normally again.

Post-Traumatic Stress is sometimes described as the experience of not wanting to remember, but being unable to forget. This was an accurate description of what Carl experienced. For him, the past (his accident) was invading the present (in which there was no present danger). Sometimes those struggling with PTS feel held hostage by the worst moments from their pasts. But thankfully, PTS doesn't have the last word. Carl now knows there is hope that these experiences can fade and even be redeemed for good.

As he worked with his biblical counselor and his Transformation Team in the manner described in this book, Carl slowly began to have less severe and less frequent episodes. A time came when his driving was no longer haunted by the fear that he would freeze up or flashback to his traumatic incident. As a result, Carl knows he has seen God working in his life and has even been able to share the comfort, encouragement, and growth he has experienced with others who struggle in the aftermath of their own trauma.

My prayer is that you have already begun to experience growth and change. As you have surrounded yourself with a Transformation Team, come to understand the nature of PTS, implemented a Peace Plan, begun to grieve the losses you have endured, and found forgiveness for any sins you committed, I hope you have felt a loosening of the hold PTS has on your life.

It's likely that when you began this journey, you were living a very dark experience, without a lot of hope for change. You might have even questioned whether your life is worth living. But the truth is that God kept you here because he has a purpose and a plan for you yet.

POST-TRAUMATIC GROWTH

Remember the coastal cypress tree, which gets beautifully shaped by the wind and rain it encounters in its home along the coast? That is a good image to keep in mind as you consider how your suffering has shaped you and what that means for today. Since we are children of God in the process of being shaped to look more like his Son, our traumatic experiences can result in good, not evil. This doesn't mean that you should overlook the pain, the losses, or the hardship you've experienced. Instead, this is an encouragement to keep adding to your perspective on such things. There are two passages in the New Testament that alert us to God's perspective on suffering. At first they might sound strange; but hang in there, and see what God might say to you through them:

> Count it all joy, my brothers, when you meet trials of various kinds, for you know that the testing of your faith produces steadfastness. And let steadfastness have its full effect, that you may be perfect and complete, lacking in nothing. (James 1:2–4)

> Therefore, since we have been justified by faith, we have peace with God through our Lord Jesus Christ. Through him we have also obtained access by faith into this grace in which we stand, and we rejoice in hope of the glory of God. Not only that, but we rejoice in our sufferings, knowing that suffering produces endurance, and endurance produces character, and character produces hope, and hope does not put us to shame, because God's love has been poured into our hearts through the Holy Spirit who has been given to us. (Romans 5:1–5)

Did you notice that both of these passages hold out the possibility of joy even in your suffering? I realize that at first this might sound like Christians are called to *masochism*—finding pleasure in pain. But God is not asking you to find pleasure in the pain itself. Rather, he wants you to find joy and pleasure in the growth and shaping that come through the pain.

In Romans 5, Paul is saying that for the Christian, suffering produces endurance, which produces character. The latter leads to us having a firmer hope in our God and his promises that will not be disappointed. James describes the growth as steadfastness which leads us to be "perfect, complete, lacking in nothing." The Bible's word for this kind of growth is "sanctification." When you belong to Jesus, he promises that he will be at work in your life through everything to make you more like him—which is essentially what sanctification means. One hope that God offers trauma sufferers through the Bible is the happy news that a person's PTS can be reframed to become Post-Traumatic Sanctification. Our sanctification as believers—our growth and change to be more like Jesus—brings God glory and helps fulfill our purpose here on earth.

In the last chapter, I mentioned there is more than one specific answer to the question, "Why God?" That is, there are clear reasons God gives in the Bible for why he allows suffering to come into our lives. First, we mustn't lose sight of the fact that the planet is currently under the curse of sin; and as a result, terrible things sometimes happen to believers and unbelievers alike. But second, for the Christian suffering has the amazing ability to help accomplish God's good plans. A third reason God sometimes allows tragedy to touch his people comes down to this matter of sanctification—it aids our spiritual growth. For God's children, then, suffering is never wasted or purposeless. God can use all of your past experiences—the pleasant, the arduous, and even the excruciating—to mold you into the image of Jesus.

How is it possible that suffering can make you more like him? Here are a few examples of how God uses suffering to accomplish that very goal. For one, suffering often makes us more compassionate than we were before we endured it. When you are able to reach out with compassion to someone who is suffering, offering practical help in his or her need, that is evidence that God is at work in you making you more like Jesus. It signals growth.

Now, if you are like most, you have responded to your suffering with tears and great sorrow. As I mentioned in the chapter on lament, that is a good thing. But have you ever considered that weeping and sorrowing are actually "Jesus-ish" responses? Remember, Isaiah 53:3 describes Jesus as a "man of sorrows and acquainted with grief," and Hebrews 5:7 tells us that in his life on this earth he prayed with "loud cries and tears." When you share your sorrows, pain, suffering, and trauma with God by weeping, you are acting like Jesus—who wasn't afraid to be real before his Father. He wasn't intimidated by the thought of letting sad emotions out. If you've noticed that you cry now more than you did before your traumatic experiences, that does not necessarily indicate any weakness. Rather, it could be another sign that you are becoming more like Jesus. This softening will help you obey the biblical instruction for the people of God to "weep with those who weep" (Romans 12:15).

Perhaps as a result of what you've been through you have become more patient with others' weaknesses and failings because you know your own weakness all too well. Perhaps you can say that you've remained faithful to your spouse and children or job or friendships, despite your sorrow and struggle. Perhaps you are noticing less escapist behavior from yourself and are exercising more self-control. These are also indicators that you are becoming more like Jesus. The Bible calls such new attitudes and actions "the fruit of the Spirit" and tells us to "walk by the Spirit" (Galatians 5:16, 22–23). Consider asking for his help every morning, perhaps by using a simple prayer like this one:

> Father, please fill me with evidence that your Spirit is in me. I want you and others to see your love, joy, peace, patience, kindness, goodness, gentleness,

faithfulness, and self-control at work through all I do. I need your help.

In Jesus's name, Amen.

The list of ways you are becoming more like Jesus through your suffering can continue to grow throughout your remaining years. So keep an eye out for new developments in your transformation.

Who Is in Control?

Almost without exception, people who live through traumatic experiences sometimes feel as if they are completely out of control. This is a terrifying feeling, and likely you can relate to it. It is no surprise that those who want to help people suffering with PTS often attempt to restore some sense of control. The idea is that gaining a sense of control can help a person overcome those frightening feelings.

But when you really think about it, none of us has any real control over the world or exactly what we will encounter from day to day. How much more reassuring it is, then, to trust in God's control over all of life instead of relying on our routines and safeguards alone. Theologians use a big word to talk about God's ultimate control over everything. They speak of God's *sovereignty*. We see the sovereignty principle behind what Joseph said to his brothers: "You meant evil against me, but God meant it for good, to bring it about that many people should be kept alive, as they are today" (Genesis 50:20). This passage gets at the truth that the believer does not have to face things—even difficult things—as a puppet or a victim. Instead, we can know that through everything that happens to us, God is at work for our good and his glory.

Because nothing happens outside of God's sovereignty, you can be sure that nothing can separate you from God's love and care either. As you wrestle with past suffering and encounter new difficulties (as we all will), remember what Paul says in Romans about God's love. He writes, "For I am sure that neither death nor life, nor angels nor rulers, nor things present nor things to come, nor powers, nor height nor depth, nor anything else in all creation, will be able to separate us from the love of God in Christ Jesus our Lord" (Romans 8:38–39). Nothing can come between you and God's love—not people, not trauma, not even death.

Trying to regain a sense of control that you never really had will not ultimately comfort you or make you feel safe. But turning to God in faith, telling him your fears, and asking for his help will welcome the power of God into your life. When you understand that he is in control and can therefore bring about your ultimate good since you are his child, then you are positioned to see purpose for your suffering and to draw closer to him in spite of your hurt and struggle.

Turn to God for Refuge

God designed us to want to flee troubles and trials. But we aren't just to run away from things, we are made to run to someone. God is a good Father, who desires good for his children. And as a good Father, he longs for us to draw near and find peace in him when we are threatened or afraid. Over a hundred times in the book of Psalms, God describes himself as a "refuge," a "stronghold," or a "shelter." A place of safety in times of trouble. When we run to him, he offers "peace" (Philippians 4:7). This peace God gives us leaves the world baffled because it guards our hearts even as we walk through trials and wrestle with the pull of anxiety.

Often when we encounter trials and difficulty, however, we don't run to our loving Father. Instead, we seek safety in false refuges—things we turn to that promise to make us feel better and take the pain away. True, some of these might help for a moment, but in the end they fail to provide lasting peace. What they offer is temporary and fleeting—and often ultimately harmful to us and to others. The most common false refuges are substance abuse and sex. But there are many others—like shopping, overeating, gambling, or gaming that also might momentarily mask the pain or distract us from it with some pleasurable sensation. Nevertheless, they all will fail to alleviate our suffering. And they may also leave us feeling empty, shamed, and even more discouraged.

What can you do to avoid that common response to trauma that would have you seek refuge in the wrong things? Start by naming those things that draw you. Work with your counselor or trusted friend to list them. Some common ones are inherently wrong (using illicit drugs, having extramarital sex, viewing pornography, etc.). These are things to put off right away. If any one of these addictions has taken control of your life, I encourage you to take some time with your counselor to work through some biblical addiction material. I suggest Ed Welch's *Crossroads: A Step-by-Step Guide away from Addiction*.[1] Processing your trauma needs to go hand-in-hand with addiction care (when it's needed) because the two problems are related. Often, traumatic experiences drive people to addictive habits and the problems easily become intertwined and compounded.

Other false refuges might not be sinful in and of themselves; nevertheless, you may need to take a break from them in the quest to turn to God for peace during hardship. Some of the things I'm referring to here may occupy a unique place in life so that you can't completely set them aside So, if you find yourself finding refuge in food itself or sex within marriage, for instance, you'll need to address your motivation. One way to do this is to pray before engaging in the activity.

I know it sounds weird to pray before you have sex, but it is actually a great way to acknowledge the good gift that sex is by thanking the gift giver. Pray and thank God for any good gift he provides that you are about to enjoy (sex, food, a run, a TV show) and ask him to help you enjoy it but not seek shelter in it. You might also avoid going to such activities as a response when you are particularly stressed or suffering. The key is to go to the Lord *first* for shelter and peace.

Granted, this is a big subject. If you'd like to learn more, you might benefit from some of the recommended resources at the end of this book.

CONCLUSION

Your current life is in the hands of God. You are here, after your trauma, for many purposes—some of which God will show you, while others will remain a mystery. Seek to live life with him, and for him. Trust his goodness and his power. Let him be in control. And when things get hard, don't run to the false refuges to which you have become accustomed. Run to him.

QUESTIONS FOR REFLECTION, DISCUSSION, & ACTION:

1. In what specific ways did your traumatic experiences make you feel out of control? How does that impact your sense of peace, safety, and security now? Why is it helpful to remember God's sovereignty?

2. What do you typically turn to when you are having a hard day? What might change were you to go to God first instead?

Chapter 10

REORIENTING YOUR FUTURE

"Everyone else in my life would be better off without me." "I would rather be dead than to keep 'living' like this." Such sentiments plague many who struggle with PTS. The symptoms and complications that accompany it can be distressing, life-altering, and put a significant strain on relationships. While not everyone who struggles with PTS contemplates suicide, it is a concern for many. Suicide is an extreme manifestation on the spectrum of hopelessness. (If you are considering it, please reach out immediately for help. Dial 9-8-8 for the Suicide and Crisis Lifeline.)

People who have been disoriented by trauma often feel hopeless. Hopeless people don't see a future for themselves, or they only imagine a dark and painful future ahead. The lives they once hoped to live are forever lost. But as I pray you are already realizing, reorienting one's heart to align with God and what he says in his Word changes everything. As we reorient toward him, our perspective on the future shifts. Carl, Vanessa, and Javier had negative views of the future when they began their journeys. But with God's help, they re-embraced hope.

LEGACY

The song "Only Jesus" by Casting Crowns decries the idea that Christians should desire their lives to leave a legacy. While I personally embrace the sentiment that my life is about making Jesus known instead of exalting myself, the truth is that each of us will leave a legacy. What I mean is that when you pass from this earth, the people you leave behind will remember you and things about you. So the question is, what kind of legacy will you leave?

Chad Robichaux, RECON Marine, former MMA champion, and founder of the Mighty Oaks Foundation, shares that during his darkest days, one of the things that held him back from committing suicide was the knowledge that the children of those who commit suicide are far more likely to end their own lives. He couldn't bear the thought of passing on a legacy of suicide to his kids. This is one of the reasons the flagship ministry of Mighty Oaks is called the Legacy Program. In it, participants are challenged at the end of a week to consider what kind of legacy they will pass along to their children, family, friends, and others they leave behind. Will it be a legacy of hopelessness and shame, or a legacy worth imitating?

Imagine for a moment that you have passed from this earth. Do you want people to think of you as someone who was always on edge? Do you want to be remembered as one who withdrew from life and the world? As someone who was dominated by fear and his or her past? Or do you want to be remembered as someone who leaned into God in the hard moments and pressed forward with his strength? Do you want those you love to learn that hardship is a thing that shuts people down, or do you want to help them trust that it can be overcome by the power of God's Spirit, with wisdom from his Word, and with the help of his family?

PAY IT FORWARD

I've already presented two answers to the common question, "Why would God allow me to go through trauma?" I pointed out that God works through your trauma to make you more like Jesus, and he allows it to accomplish good for you that brings glory to him. A third answer is that God can use your trauma to help others. To get a sense of what I mean, read 2 Corinthians 1:3–4 slowly:

> Blessed be the God and Father of our Lord Jesus Christ, the Father of mercies and God of all comfort, who comforts us in all our affliction, so that we may be able to comfort those who are in any affliction, with the comfort with which we ourselves are comforted by God.

Our suffering can be a catalyst that makes us turn to God for comfort, which we don't tend to seek when everything in life feels just fine. And the comfort that he provides when we go to him doesn't just help us cope with a particular moment or situation. Rather, it prepares us to be able to pay comfort forward when we encounter others who suffer.

Without exception, every person disoriented by trauma whom I've counseled found some peace in the knowledge that their pain could be used to help others in the way I'm advocating. Sharing about what we've walked through with God's help adds purpose to our pain. No, it doesn't take the pain away, but it helps us bear it, to find significance in it, and even be thankful for it.

In my own ministry, people have opened up to me about unspeakable things they had not shared with anyone before, or only with a select few. And in many cases they did so because I shared my own story of trauma first. While I wouldn't wish my worst moments on anyone else, I have come to be thankful for them in a way. Certainly not because of the events themselves but for the fruit that has been born out of that suffering. I pray the Lord brings you to a point where you can say the same one day. I can certainly testify that the comfort he provides grows exponentially greater as you share with other sufferers about what God has done for you and see them begin to experience some of the same.

PURPOSE

Trauma can seem to steal purpose from our lives. But as you reorient your life around God and what his Word teaches, you will witness these purposeful realities for yourself:

1. Experiencing trauma can make us more like Jesus over time.
2. Experiencing trauma can bring glory and honor to God in the long run.
3. Experiencing trauma can prepare us to offer other sufferers help and hope.

There are many specific ways these realities can manifest, and there are many more reasons for what God brings into your life than you or I could begin to guess. But what I want you to embrace fully is that everything you have been through—including your traumatic experiences—has purpose, meaning, and significance beyond what you can see today. And that means your future is hopeful and bright. You have no idea what kind of positive things and blessings await you! You don't know how different your life might look a few years from now. You can't yet fathom how many lives will be blessed by yours. But as long as there is blood pumping through your veins and breath flowing through your lungs, God is working out beautiful plans in and through you, his child because of your faith in Jesus. In Philippians 1:6 Paul underscores this reality. He promises that "[God] who began a good work in you will bring it to completion at the day of Jesus Christ." He will keep at the work of transforming you to be more and more like his Son until you see Jesus face-to-face (1 John 3:2).

No one can promise you a future free of trial. I can't guarantee that your bad memories will go away, that you will never have another nightmare, or that the path forward will be easy either. But I can promise you that God is at work, and he is molding you to be the man or woman he wants you to be. Moreover, your life story is part of God's larger story—his grand narrative of redemptive history.

The Bible portrays a cosmic battle between good and evil in which there are villains but also heroes. And Jesus, the ultimate hero, gave up his life (and then took it up again) for those he loves. This act of sacrificial love is so potent that news of it draws many who were once his enemies to become his allies. And they, in turn, can spend their own lives as heroes, loving sacrificially so that still more choose to trust in and follow Jesus as well. Readers of Scripture know that in the end, all evil will be defeated and Jesus Christ's everlasting kingdom of peace, love, and joy will be established physically forever (Revelation 21). Until then, though, there will be pain, suffering, and death until the chief enemy, Satan, is finally vanquished. Happily, in this particular act of history, the way you and I live has eternal significance. We really can help in the critical work of encouraging others to accept that he is the way home, as well as humanity's greatest comfort in the meantime.

When gazing up at the night sky in a remote part of the world, you can see innumerable points of light shining down. All those stars are truly a majestic and beautiful sight. Each point of light contributes to the masterpiece. But have you ever noticed that most of the night sky is not occupied by lights but by the black emptiness between the stars? Without this backdrop, we could not see the lights. Similarly, only when it is set against the black backdrop of suffering can the light within you—the light of Jesus—shine forth at full brilliance.

QUESTIONS FOR REFLECTION, DISCUSSION, & ACTION:

1. Think about what kind of legacy you want to leave for your family and friends. How do you want people to remember you? How might your upcoming choices help to shape their lives positively?

2. Have you had the chance to help someone because of the suffering you have lived through? If so, how did that influence the way you think about your trauma?

3. Which of God's purposes for suffering that've been presented in this book means the most to you? Why?

Resource 1

TRANSFORMATION TEAM ADDITIONS

In chapter 1 I described a number of roles within a group called the Transformation Team. This current resource covers a few additional members that a counselor, for whom I included "A Word for the Helper" in the introduction, may also want to invite into the care process if needed.

CO-COUNSELOR

In certain situations, it is ideal to have a co-counselor working with the primary biblical counselor. This person, too, will need to be trained as a biblical counselor who will join the counseling sessions and offer insight and wisdom in the midst of them. Using a co-counselor is not always necessary but here are some examples of situations in which it might be advisable. First, it is helpful when counseling a couple in which both parties have been disoriented by trauma. Having a female counselor for the wife and a male counselor for the husband, who can meet individually with them and also jointly when they are in session as a couple can prove a huge benefit. This approach is also helpful when you are counseling someone of the opposite gender. Having a co-counselor is not a requirement in such cases, but it is helpful to have someone of the same gender as the person receiving care participate in the counseling process. Third, a co-counselor is a major benefit on particularly challenging, difficult, or weighty cases. Sometimes it is good for the counselor to have another trained caregiver there who can help make wise decisions. Co-counselors can also be a source of encouragement for one another as they jointly bear the burdens of those they care for (Galatians 6:1–2).

DEDICATED CO-SUFFERER

A dedicated co-sufferer is someone who has been through trauma in the past, received care, has experienced some degree of post-traumatic sanctification, and is willing to speak about it. He or she does not have to be a trained biblical counselor or to have completely resolved all issues related to past trauma. This person needs only be available to come to one or two sessions of counseling to share his or her testimony of God's work in and through the trauma personally endured. The testimony of the co-sufferer helps put flesh on the truths of God's Word. This can help the person who is currently disoriented by trauma know he or she is not alone, that there is help, hope, reason to move forward, and the potential for a future ahead. A co-sufferer such as I advocate here is not always necessary, but if the person receiving care has trouble believing what God's Word says about his or her personal circumstances, then I do highly recommend bringing a co-sufferer in for at least one session.

If you as the primary counselor, co-counselor, or ally have been through trauma and experienced post-traumatic sanctification to the point where you can share from your story, you can demonstrate these truths without having a separate co-sufferer involved.

RESIDENTIAL PROGRAMS

For veterans and first responders struggling with PTS and their spouses, the Mighty Oaks Foundation offers the Legacy Program, a free weeklong intensive experience. Find out more at mightyoaksprograms.org.

For men struggling with substance abuse, consider one of the following residential biblical counseling programs:

Restoration: faithlafayette.org/restoration, restorationministry@faithlafayette.org

The Damascus House: thedamascushouse.com

The Refuge: refugewinterset.com

For women who struggle with substance abuse, consider one of these:

The Damascus House: thedamascushouse.com

Vision of Hope: faithlafayette.org/voh, voh@faithlafayette.org

IN CASE OF EMERGENCY

Don't neglect the valuable resources available like 911 or 988 (the Suicide and Crisis Lifeline). If someone is a threat to themselves or others, please take advantage of these resources.

In cases of abuse,* encourage the one being abused to utilize these resources: National Domestic Violence Hotline at 800-799-7233 or by texting START to 88788.

Also see Called to Peace: www.calledtopeace.org.

* This book is not intended to offer training for counseling abuse. If you would like more training on abuse counseling, contact the ministry above or read *Is It Abuse?: A Biblical Guide to Identifying Domestic Abuse and Helping Victims* by Darby A. Strickland.

Resource 2
TRIGGER LOG

Soon after you experience any triggering event, take some time to answer these questions (consider taking a picture of them or creating a note with them on your phone). You can write or type up your answers on a separate piece of paper or record them on your phone. Share them with your counselor or trusted friends who can help you identify currently unknown patterns that may contribute to triggering you.

1. Where was I?
2. What time was it?
3. Who else was there (which individuals or groups)?
4. What did I see?
5. What was I hearing?
6. Were there any scents that stood out?
7. Were there any textures that I recall strongly?
8. What bodily sensations did I experience?
9. What reaction did I have (a flashback, a zone-out, a black out, etc.)?
10. Did I make any active response to the situation (try to remove myself from the situation, execute Peace Plan, reach out for help, etc.)?
11. How did the episode resolve?
12. How long did the episode last?

Resource 3
HEART CHARTS

The following are helpful tools for you and your counselor to use in gaining access to what's going on in your soul. Feel free to make copies of these charts, or draw them out on blank pieces of paper. My hope is that as you are meeting with someone with relation to the topics discussed in this book that you'll be sure to fill out at least one of each throughout your meetings. The chart entitled "My Past Past," should not change unless you recall more details of what you experience as you move forward. How you fill out the other charts will likely change over time as you grow and change.

MY PAST PAST

Fill out the table below with the most pronounced or first reactions regarding each of these categories as they relate to your past experiences. Try to list the thoughts, feelings, and desires you had toward each of these categories *at the time of your traumatic experience*. If you did not have any, leave it blank. (For instance, if you did not have any thoughts, feelings, or desires about God in the moments that led to your trauma, do not fill it in.)

	Thoughts/ Beliefs (Cognition)	Choices/Desires (Volition)	Emotions (Affection)
God			
Others			
Myself			
Circum-stances			

MY PRESENT PAST

As you fill out this chart with relation to your past trauma, put down the first things that come to mind right now. The goal is to list your present thoughts, feelings, and desires related to the past.

	Thoughts/ Beliefs (Cognition)	Choices/Desires (Volition)	Emotions (Affection)
God			
Others			
Myself			
Circum- stances			

MY REORIENTED PAST

This chart should be filled out after you have spent some time studying what God's Word says about himself, you, and your suffering, preferably with a trusted friend or biblical counselor. As you fill out this chart with relation to your past trauma, put down the first things that come to mind after they have been influenced by God's Word.

	Thoughts/ Beliefs (Cognition)	Choices/Desires (Volition)	Emotions (Affection)
God			
Others			
Myself			
Circum-stances			

MY PRESENT

Fill out the table below with the most pronounced or first reactions regarding each of these categories related to your present life.

	Thoughts/ Beliefs (Cognition)	Choices/Desires (Volition)	Emotions (Affection)
God			
Others			
Myself			
Circum-stances			

MY FUTURE

Fill out the table below with the most pronounced or first reactions regarding each of these categories as you consider your future.

	Thoughts/ Beliefs (Cognition)	Choices/Desires (Volition)	Emotions (Affection)
God			
Others			
Myself			
Circum-stances			

MY SUFFERING

Fill out the table below with the most pronounced or first reactions regarding each of these categories related to a specific trial in your life.

	Thoughts/ Beliefs (Cognition)	Choices/Desires (Volition)	Emotions (Affection)
God			
Others			
Myself			
Circum-stances			

Resource 4

WHO I AM TO CHRIST[1]

- I am of value and share the same heavenly Father with him (Matthew 6:26).
- I am one worth seeking when I feel lost (Matthew 18:10–14).
- I am his spiritual sibling (Mark 3:34–35).
- I am, like him, a child of the Most High God (Luke 6:35).
- I am his friend (Luke 12:4).
- I am one (re)born of the Spirit (John 3:6).
- I am one so loved by the Father that Jesus, his only begotten Son, died for me so that I could live with him forever (John 3:16).
- I am eternally his, secure in God's holy love (John 10:28–30).
- I am a branch abiding in him, the vine. With his help, I can bear good fruit (John 15:5).
- I am his love (John 15:9).
- I am one forgiven because I believe in him (Acts 10:43).
- I am one obtained at the price of his shed blood (Acts 20:28).
- Together with all other true believers, I am God's church and, biblically speaking, a saint (Acts 20:28; 1 Corinthians 1:2).

- I am one whose sins are no longer counted (Romans 4:7–8).
- I am one at peace with God (Romans 5:1; Ephesians 2:14–17).
- I am one with confident, bold access to God thanks to him (Romans 5:2; Ephesians 2:18–22).
- I am one with the love of God poured into my heart (Romans 5:15).
- I am one of the saved, those delivered from God's wrath (Romans 5:9).
- I am one reconciled to God (Romans 5:10–11).
- I am one who can cry, "Abba, Daddy" to God (Romans 8:15).
- I am his joint-heir (Romans 8:17).
- I am one whom God is for (Romans 8:31).
- I am one chosen by grace (Romans 11:5).
- I am one he welcomes (Romans 15:7).
- I, together with all the other saints, am his body (1 Corinthians 12:27; Ephesians 4:12; 5:23).
- I am one sealed by the Spirit (2 Corinthians 1:22).
- I am betrothed to him as his pure bride (2 Corinthians 11:2).
- I am Abraham's spiritual offspring (Galatians 3:29).
- I am one set free from slavery to sin (Galatians 4:7).
- I am one chosen to be blameless and holy and was predestined to be adopted into God's family (Ephesians 1:4–6).
- I am one who has been redeemed (Ephesians 1:7).
- I am God's masterpiece, created to do the good works he prepared just for me (Ephesians 2:10).
- I am one now near to God via his blood (Ephesians 2:13).
- I, together with all believers, am a citizen of God's household (Ephesians 2:19).
- I am part of the dwelling place in which God lives by his Spirit (Ephesians 2:22).

- I am one who can be filled with the fullness of God (Ephesians 3:19).
- I am one he nourishes and cherishes (Ephesians 5:29).
- I am one whose sins are remembered no more (Hebrews 8:12).
- I am one with a good, clear conscience before God (1 Peter 3:21).
- I, together with all believers, am his bride (Revelation 19:7).

RECOMMENDED RESOURCES ON POST-TRAUMATIC STRESS

Articles

- Michael R. Emlet, "Let Me Draw a Picture: Understanding the Influences on the Human Heart," *The Journal of Biblical Counseling* 20, no. 2 (2002): 47–58.
- Sethanne Howard and Mark W. Crandall, "Post Traumatic Stress Disorder What Happens in the Brain?" *Journal of the Washington Academy of Sciences* 93, no. 3 (Fall 2007): 1–17.
- Robert Jones, "Distinguishing Between Guilt and Guilt," *Biblical Counseling Coalition* (blog), July 18, 2017, http://biblicalcounselingcoalition.org/2017/07/18/distinguishing-between-guilt-and-guilt/.
- Robert Kellemen, "Biblical Counseling Coalition | Who I Am To Christ," Biblical Counseling Coalition, March 14, 2012, https://www.biblicalcounselingcoalition.org/2012/03/14/who-i-am-to-christ/.
- Paul Randolph, "Post-Traumatic Distress," *The Journal of Biblical Counseling* 25, no. 3 (Summer 2007).

- Curtis W. Solomon, "Counseling Post-Traumatic Stress Disorder: Plotting the Course," *ACBC Essays* 2 (2019): 43–56.

Books

- Barrett Craig, *Help! I've Been Traumatized by Combat* (Wapwallopen, PA: Shepherd Press, 2015).
- Robert W. Kellemen, *God's Healing for Life's Losses: How to Find Hope When You're Hurting* (Winona Lake, IN: BMH Books, 2010).
- Jeremy Lelek, *Post-Traumatic Stress Disorder: Recovering Hope* (Phillipsburg, NJ: P&R Publishing, 2013).
- Jeremy Pierre, *The Dynamic Heart in Daily Life: Connecting Christ to Human Experience* (Greensboro, NC: New Growth Press, 2016).
- David Powlison, *Good and Angry: Redeeming Anger, Irritation, Complaining, and Bitterness* (Greensboro, NC: New Growth Press, 2016).
- Chad M. Robichaux, *An Unfair Advantage: Victory in The Midst of Battle* (Manassas, VA: Making Life Better Publishing, 2017).
- Chad M. Robichaux and Jeremy M. Stalnecker, *The Truth About PTSd* (Manassas, VA: Making Life Better Publishing, 2017).
- Chad M. Robichaux, Jeremy M. Stalnecker, and John A. Mizerak, *Path to Resiliency* (Manassas, VA: Making Life Better Publishing, 2017).
- Stephen Viars, *Putting Your Past in Its Place* (Eugene: Harvest House Publishers, 2011).
- Mark Vroegop, *Dark Clouds, Deep Mercy: Discovering the Grace of Lament* (Wheaton, IL: Crossway, 2019).

Lectures and Conference Talks

- Chad Robichaux, "Personal Testimony," (lecture presented at the 2015 Men's Advance of Cornerstone Community Church, Atascadero, CA, September 12, 2015).
- Joni Eareckson Tada, "Emotions in the Face of Suffering," (presented at the CCEF National Conference, Chattanooga, TN, October 14, 2016).

Support Programs

- Fallen Soldiers March, which offers free biblical counseling to veterans (https://fallensoldiersmarch.com/)
- GriefShare (https://www.griefshare.org/)
- Mighty Oaks Foundation (https://www.mightyoaksprograms.org/)

Training for Counselors

- For trauma counseling training, visit https://solomonsoulcare.com/training/.

ENDNOTES

Chapter 1

1. I prefer to use PTS or PTSd over PTSD (Post-Traumatic Stress Disorder) for a variety of reasons I will explain later. I will use PTSD to refer to a diagnosis someone has received, but PTS to describe the common phenomenon experienced by those who have been through severe suffering.

2. To find out more, visit https://www.mightyoaksprograms.org/.

3. Joni Eareckson Tada, "Emotions in the Face of Suffering," October 14, 2016, CCEF National Conference, Chattanooga, TN.

4. In addition to the Transformation Team members suggested in this chapter, there are some others that may prove helpful. See Resource 1.

5. Examples of this use include Luke 22:28; Acts 20:19; Galatians 4:14; James 1:2, 12; 1 Peter 1:6; 2 Peter 2:9; and Revelation 3:10.

6. Visit https://www.mightyoaksprograms.org/.

7. Visit https://www.griefshare.org.

Chapter 2

1. Frank W. Weathers and Terence M. Keane, "The Criterion A Problem Revisited: Controversies and Challenges in Defining and Measuring Psychological Trauma," *Journal of*

Traumatic Stress 20, no. 2 (April 2007): 271–72; *Diagnostic and Statistical Manual of Mental Disorders: DSM-5* (Washington, DC: American Psychiatric Association, 2013), 271.

2. Barrett Craig, *Help! I've Been Traumatized by Combat* (Wapwallopen, PA: Shepherd Press, 2015), 4–5, 10, 53; Paul Randolph, "Post-Traumatic Distress," *The Journal of Biblical Counseling* 25, no. 3 (Summer 2007): 11; Curtis W. Solomon, "Counseling Post-Traumatic Stress Disorder: Plotting the Course," *ACBC Essays* 2 (2019): 44–47. The exact terminology used by people who disagree with the PTSD label is varied, but we all agree with the principle.

3. The following section is a condensation of information from the following sources. Gino L. Collura and Daniel H. Lende, "Post-Traumatic Stress Disorder and Neuroanthropology: Stopping PTSD Before It Begins," *Annals of Anthropological Practice* 36, no. 1 (May 2012): 131–48; J. Douglas Bremner, *Does Stress Damage the Brain? Understanding Trauma-Related Disorders from a Mind-Body Perspective* (New York: W.W. Norton, 2002); Bessel A. Van der Kolk, *The Body Keeps the Score: Brain, Mind, and Body in the Healing of Trauma* (New York: Penguin Books, 2015); Sethanne Howard and Mark W. Crandall, "Post Traumatic Stress Disorder What Happens in the Brain?," *Journal of the Washington Academy of Sciences* 93, no. 3 (Fall 2007): 1–17; Benno Roozendaal, Bruce S. McEwen, and Sumantra Chattarji, "Stress, Memory and the Amygdala," *Nature Reviews Neuroscience* 10, no. 6 (June 2009): 423–33; Emily B. Ansell et al., "Cumulative Adversity and Smaller Gray Matter Volume in Medial Prefrontal, Anterior Cingulate, and Insula Regions," *Biological Psychiatry* 72, no. 1 (July 1, 2012): 57–64; Rand S. Swenson, "Chapter 9: Limbic System," in *Review of Clinical and Functional Neuroscience* (Hanover, NH: Dartmouth Medical School, 2006); Rand S. Swenson, "Chapter 10: The Thalamus," in *Review of Clinical and Functional Neuroscience* (Hanover, NH: Dartmouth Medical School, 2006); Sara Antunes-Alves and Thea Comeau, "A Clinician's Guide to the Neurobiology

Underlying the Presentation and Treatment of PTSD and Subsequent Growth," *Archives of Psychiatry & Psychotherapy* 16, no. 3 (September 2014): 9–17; Amy F. T. Arnsten et al., "The Effects of Stress Exposure on Prefrontal Cortex: Translating Basic Research into Successful Treatments for Post-Traumatic Stress Disorder," *Neurobiology of Stress* 1 (October 27, 2014): 89–99; Einat Levy-Gigi et al., "Association among Clinical Response, Hippocampal Volume, and FKBP5 Gene Expression in Individuals with Posttraumatic Stress Disorder Receiving Cognitive Behavioral Therapy," *Biological Psychiatry* 74, no. 11 (December 1, 2013): 793–800; Erik B. Bloss et al., "Evidence for Reduced Experience-Dependent Dendritic Spine Plasticity in the Aging Prefrontal Cortex," *Journal of Neuroscience* 31, no. 21 (May 25, 2011): 7831–39; no. 1 (May 2012) H. Barbas et al., "Relationship of Prefrontal Connections to Inhibitory Systems in Superior Temporal Areas in the Rhesus Monkey," *Cerebral Cortex* 15, no. 9 (September 1, 2005): 1368.

4. See Van der Kolk, *The Body Keeps the Score*, 82–83; Howard and Crandall, "Post Traumatic Stress Disorder What Happens in the Brain?," 13.

5. Van der Kolk, *The Body Keeps the Score*, 60–69; Howard and Crandall, "Post Traumatic Stress Disorder What Happens in the Brain?," 11–12; Swenson, "Chapter 9: Limbic System," 3–4; Yana Lokshina and Israel Liberzon, "Enhancing Efficacy of PTSD Treatment: Role of Circuits, Genetics, and Optimal Timing," *Clinical Psychology: Science & Practice* 24, no. 3 (September 2017): 299; Arnsten et al., "The Effects of Stress Exposure on Prefrontal Cortex," 90.

6. Van der Kolk, *The Body Keeps the Score*, 54, 62.

7. I prefer to use improper involuntary external threat response initiation stimuli (IEITRIS) instead of using the word *triggered*, but—for perhaps obvious reasons—that hasn't caught on.

8. Arnsten et al., "The Effects of Stress Exposure on Prefrontal Cortex."

9. Chad Robichaux, "Personal Testimony," September 12, 2015, Men's Advance of Cornerstone Community Church, Atascadero, CA.

10. Levy-Gigi et al., "Association among Clinical Response, Hippocampal Volume, and FKBP5 Gene Expression in Individuals with Posttraumatic Stress Disorder Receiving Cognitive Behavioral Therapy"; Arnsten et al., "The Effects of Stress Exposure on Prefrontal Cortex"; Ansell et al., "Cumulative Adversity and Smaller Gray Matter Volume in Medial Prefrontal, Anterior Cingulate, and Insula Regions."

Chapter 3

1. The concept of God's original design plan is drawn from the writings of Alvin Plantinga's epistemological works. See Alvin Plantinga, *Warrant and Proper Function* (New York: Oxford University Press, 1993); *Warranted Christian Belief* (New York: Oxford University Press, 2000); and *Warrant: The Current Debate* (New York: Oxford University Press, 1993).

2. This diagram is an amalgamation of ideas from a variety of places, including Jeremy Pierre, *The Dynamic Heart in Daily Life: Connecting Christ to Human Experience* (Greensboro, NC: New Growth Press, 2016); Michael R. Emlet, "Let Me Draw a Picture: Understanding the Influences on the Human Heart," *The Journal of Biblical Counseling* 20, no. 2 (2002): 47–58. I also consulted a diagram from David Powlison that was recounted by David T. Harvey in *I Still Do: Growing Closer and Stronger through Life's Defining Moments* (Grand Rapids: Baker Books, 2020), 69.

Chapter 4

1. Dissociative episodes are instances in which a person's inner-person state (thoughts, emotions memories, etc.) do not coincide with external reality. With PTS these episodes are typically connected with remembering or reliving a traumatic

experience. The person may just zone out or could physically act out behaviors related to the traumatic memory.

2. Po-Han Chou et al., "Panic Disorder and Risk of Stroke: A Population-Based Study," *Psychosomatics* 53, no. 5 (September 1, 2012): 463–69, https://doi.org/10.1016/j.psym.2012.03.007; Una D. McCann, "Anxiety and Heart Disease," October 15, 2021, https://www.hopkinsmedicine.org/health/conditions-and-diseases/anxiety-and-heart-disease.

3. This practice may remind some readers of Exposure Therapy. Exposure Therapy offers very specific practices for exposing people to triggers or things they fear which I am not prescribing. Both my counsel and Exposure Therapy recognize the long-understood value of facing one's fears as a part of overcoming them. My intent is neither to critique nor condone Exposure Therapy in this work. If you want to learn more about exposure therapy, see Edna B. Foa, Elizabeth Ann Hembree, and Barbara Olasov Rothbaum, *Prolonged Exposure Therapy for PTSD: Emotional Processing of Traumatic Experiences: Therapist Guide*, Treatments That Work (New York: Oxford University Press, 2007).

Chapter 5

1. See Elizabeth Kubler-Ross, *On Death and Dying* (New York: Scribner, reissue edition, 2014) and Elizabeth Kubler-Ross and David Kessler, *On Grief and Grieving* (New York: Scribner, reprint edition, 2014).

2. Robert W. Kellemen, *God's Healing for Life's Losses: How to Find Hope When You're Hurting* (Winona Lake, IN: BMH Books, 2010), 16.

3. Mark Vroegop, *Dark Clouds, Deep Mercy: Discovering the Grace of Lament* (Wheaton, IL: Crossway, 2019), 30.; Kellemen, *God's Healing for Life's Losses*, 31–36.

4. Vroegop, *Dark Clouds, Deep Mercy,* 21.

5. Kellemen, *God's Healing for Life's Losses*, 18.

6. Vroegop, *Dark Clouds, Deep Mercy,* 26.

Chapter 6

1. Edward T. Welch, *Shame Interrupted* (Greensboro, NC: New Growth Press, 2012), 2.

2. Robert Jones, "Distinguishing Between Guilt and Guilt," *Biblical Counseling Coalition* (blog), July 18, 2017, https://www.biblicalcounselingcoalition.org/2017/07/18/distinguishing-between-guilt-and-guilt/.

3. Stephen Viars, *Putting Your Past in Its Place* (Eugene, OR: Harvest House Publishers, 2011).

4. "Read Rachael Denhollander's Full Victim Impact Statement about Larry Nassar | CNN," accessed March 19, 2023, https://www.cnn.com/2018/01/24/us/rachael-denhollander-full-statement/index.html; *Victim Rachael Denhollander Confronts Nassar*, 2018, https://www.youtube.com/watch?v=-8jUCrPArHQ; Murray Campbell, "Rachael Denhollander and Her Extraordinary Speech," The Gospel Coalition | Australia, January 25, 2018, https://au.thegospelcoalition.org/article/rachael-denhollander-extraordinary-speech/.

5. David Powlison, *Good and Angry: Redeeming Anger, Irritation, Complaining, and Bitterness* (Greensboro, NC: New Growth Press, 2016), 80–87.

Chapter 7

1. Stephen J. Lepore and Tracey A. Revenson, "Resilience and Posttraumatic Growth: Recovery, Resistance, and Reconfiguration," in *Handbook of Posttraumatic Growth: Research and Practice* (New York: Lawrence Erlbaum Associates, 2006), 25–27.

Chapter 8

1. This chart is included in the *Transformation Bible Study Journal*. It is available for purchase at https://solomonsoulcare.com/product/transformation-bible-study-journal/.

2. Joni Eareckson Tada, *The God I Love: A Lifetime of Walking with Jesus* (Grand Rapids: Zondervan, 2009), 9.

Chapter 9

1. Edward T. Welch, *Crossroads: A Step-by-Step Guide away from Addiction* (Greensboro, NC: New Growth Press, 2008).

Resource 4

1. Robert Kellemen, "Biblical Counseling Coalition | Who I Am To Christ," Biblical Counseling Coalition, March 14, 2012, https://www.biblicalcounselingcoalition.org/2012/03/14/who-i-am-to-christ/.

BIBLIOGRAPHY

American Psychiatric Association and DSM-5 Task Force. *Diagnostic and Statistical Manual of Mental Disorders: DSM-5.* Washington, DC: American Psychiatric Association, 2013.

Ansell, Emily B., Kenneth Rando, Keri Tuit, Joseph Guarnaccia, and Rajita Sinha. "Cumulative Adversity and Smaller Gray Matter Volume in Medial Prefrontal, Anterior Cingulate, and Insula Regions." *Biological Psychiatry* 72, no. 1 (July 1, 2012): 57–64.

Antunes-Alves, Sara, and Thea Comeau. "A Clinician's Guide to the Neurobiology Underlying the Presentation and Treatment of PTSD and Subsequent Growth." *Archives of Psychiatry & Psychotherapy* 16, no. 3 (September 2014): 9–17.

"Anxiety and Heart Disease," October 15, 2021. https://www.hopkinsmedicine.org/health/conditions-and-diseases/anxiety-and-heart-disease.

Arnsten, Amy F. T., Murray A. Raskind, Fletcher B. Taylor, and Daniel F. Connor. "The Effects of Stress Exposure on Prefrontal Cortex: Translating Basic Research into Successful Treatments for Post-Traumatic Stress Disorder." *Neurobiology of Stress* 1 (October 27, 2014): 89–99.

Bloss, Erik B., William G. Janssen, Daniel T. Ohm, Frank J. Yuk, Shannon Wadsworth, Karl M. Saardi, Bruce S. McEwen, and John H. Morrison. "Evidence for Reduced Experience-Dependent Dendritic Spine Plasticity in the Aging Prefrontal Cortex." *Journal of Neuroscience* 31, no. 21 (May 25, 2011): 7831–39.

Bremner, J. Douglas. *Does Stress Damage the Brain? Understanding Trauma-Related Disorders from a Mind-Body Perspective*. New York: W.W. Norton, 2002.

Campbell, Murray. "Rachael Denhollander and Her Extraordinary Speech." The Gospel Coalition | Australia, January 25, 2018. https://au.thegospelcoalition.org/article/rachael-denhollander-extraordinary-speech/.

Chou, Po-Han, Ching-Heng Lin, El-Wui Loh, Chin-Hong Chan, and Tsuo-Hung Lan. "Panic Disorder and Risk of Stroke: A Population-Based Study." *Psychosomatics* 53, no. 5 (September 1, 2012): 463–69. https://doi.org/10.1016/j.psym.2012.03.007.

Collura, Gino L., and Daniel H. Lende. "Post-Traumatic Stress Disorder and Neuroanthropology: Stopping Ptsd Before It Begins." *Annals of Anthropological Practice* 36, no. 1 (May 2012): 131–48.

Craig, Barrett. *Help! I've Been Traumatized by Combat*. Wapwallopen, PA: Shepherd Press, 2015.

Eareckson Tada, Joni. "Emotions in the Face of Suffering." Presented at the CCEF National Conference, Chattanooga, TN, October 14, 2016.

Emlet, Michael R. "Let Me Draw a Picture: Understanding the Influences on the Human Heart." *The Journal of Biblical Counseling* 20, no. 2 (2002): 47–58.

Foa, Edna B., Elizabeth Ann Hembree, and Barbara Olasov Rothbaum. *Prolonged Exposure Therapy for PTSD: Emotional Processing of Traumatic Experiences: Therapist Guide*.

Treatments That Work. New York: Oxford University Press, 2007.

Harvey, David T. *I Still Do: Growing Closer and Stronger through Life's Defining Moments*. Grand Rapids: Baker Books, 2020.

Howard, Sethanne, and Mark W. Crandall. "Post Traumatic Stress Disorder What Happens in the Brain?" *Journal of the Washington Academy of Sciences* 93, no. 3 (Fall 2007): 1–17.

Jones, Robert. "Distinguishing Between Guilt and Guilt." *Biblical Counseling Coalition* (blog), July 18, 2017. http://biblicalcounselingcoalition.org/2017/07/18/distinguishing-between-guilt-and-guilt/.

Kellemen, Robert. "Biblical Counseling Coalition | Who I Am To Christ." Biblical Counseling Coalition, March 14, 2012. https://www.biblicalcounselingcoalition.org/2012/03/14/who-i-am-to-christ/.

———. *God's Healing for Life's Losses: How to Find Hope When You're Hurting*. Winona Lake, IN: BMH Books, 2010.

Lepore, Stephen J., and Tracey A. Revenson. "Resilience and Posttraumatic Growth: Recovery, Resistance, and Reconfiguration." In *Handbook of Posttraumatic Growth: Research and Practice*, 24–46. New York: Lawrence Erlbaum Associates, 2006.

Levy-Gigi, Einat, Csilla Szabó, Oguz Kelemen, and Szabolcs Kéri. "Association among Clinical Response, Hippocampal Volume, and FKBP5 Gene Expression in Individuals with Posttraumatic Stress Disorder Receiving Cognitive Behavioral Therapy." *Biological Psychiatry* 74, no. 11 (December 1, 2013): 793–800.

Lokshina, Yana, and Israel Liberzon. "Enhancing Efficacy of PTSD Treatment: Role of Circuits, Genetics, and Optimal

Timing." *Clinical Psychology: Science & Practice* 24, no. 3 (September 2017): 298–301.

Pierre, Jeremy. *The Dynamic Heart in Daily Life: Connecting Christ to Human Experience*. Greensboro, NC: New Growth Press, 2016.

Plantinga, Alvin. *Warrant and Proper Function*. New York: Oxford University Press, 1993.

———. *Warrant: The Current Debate*. New York: Oxford University Press, 1993.

———. *Warranted Christian Belief*. New York: Oxford University Press, 2000.

Powlison, David. *Good and Angry: Redeeming Anger, Irritation, Complaining, and Bitterness*. Greensboro, NC: New Growth Press, 2016.

Randolph, Paul. "Post-Traumatic Distress." *The Journal of Biblical Counseling* 25, no. 3 (Summer 2007).

"Read Rachael Denhollander's Full Victim Impact Statement about Larry Nassar | CNN." Accessed March 19, 2023. https://www.cnn.com/2018/01/24/us/rachael-denhollander-full-statement/index.html.

Robichaux, Chad. "Personal Testimony." Lecture presented at the 2015 Men's Advance of Cornerstone Community Church, Atascadero, CA, September 12, 2015.

Roozendaal, Benno, Bruce S. McEwen, and Sumantra Chattarji. "Stress, Memory and the Amygdala." *Nature Reviews Neuroscience* 10, no. 6 (June 2009): 423–33.

Solomon, Curtis W. "Counseling Post-Traumatic Stress Disorder: Plotting the Course." *ACBC Essays* 2 (2019): 43–56.

Swenson, Rand S. "Chapter 9: Limbic System." In *Review of Clinical and Functional Neuroscience*, Online Version. Hanover, NH: Dartmouth Medical School, 2006. https://

www.dartmouth.edu/~rswenson/NeuroSci/chapter_9.html.

———. "Chapter 10: The Thalamus." In *Review of Clinical and Functional Neuroscience*, Online Version. Hanover, NH: Dartmouth Medical School, 2006. https://www.dartmouth.edu/~rswenson/NeuroSci/chapter_9.html.

Van der Kolk, Bessel A. *The Body Keeps the Score: Brain, Mind, and Body in the Healing of Trauma*. New York: Penguin Books, 2015.

Viars, Stephen. *Putting Your Past in Its Place*. Eugene: Harvest House Publishers, 2011.

Victim Rachael Denhollander Confronts Nassar, 2018. https://www.youtube.com/watch?v=-8jUCrPArHQ.

Vroegop, Mark. *Dark Clouds, Deep Mercy: Discovering the Grace of Lament*. Wheaton, IL: Crossway, 2019.

Weathers, Frank W., and Terence M. Keane. "The Criterion A Problem Revisited: Controversies and Challenges in Defining and Measuring Psychological Trauma." *Journal of Traumatic Stress* 20, no. 2 (April 2007): 107–21.